Drupal Intranets with Open Atrium

Discover an intranet solution for your organization with Open Atrium

Tracy Charles Smith

[PACKT] open source
PUBLISHING
community experience distilled

BIRMINGHAM - MUMBAI

Drupal Intranets with Open Atrium

First published: January 2011

Production Reference: 1281210

Published by Packt Publishing Ltd.
32 Lincoln Road
Olton
Birmingham, B27 6PA, UK.

ISBN 978-1-849511-12-4

www.packtpub.com

Cover Image by Faiz Fattohi (Filosarti@tiscali.it)

Credits

Author
Tracy Charles Smith

Reviewers
Dave Poon

Floris van Woudenberg

Acquisition Editor
Dilip Venkatesh

Development Editor
Wilson D'souza

Technical Editor
Azharuddin Sheikh

Copy Editor
Neha Shetty

Indexer
Monica Ajmera Mehta

Editorial Team Leader
Akshara Aware

Project Team Leader
Ashwin Shetty

Project Coordinator
Michelle Quadros

Proofreader
Aaron Nash

Graphics
Nilesh Mohite

Production Coordinator
Kruthika Bangera

Cover Work
Kruthika Bangera

About the Author

Tracy Charles Smith began working with computers at the age of 10. Tracy's experience includes Network Integration, Database Design, ColdFusion, and PHP programming. Tracy received his B.S. in Computer Information Systems and Business Administration from Wingate University. After graduating from college, Tracy worked in the Network Management and Telecommunications fields for several years. While he enjoyed network support and designing networks, he wanted to shift his focus towards programming. He joined a small startup named PrizeCentral.com as a Senior Programmer. PrizeCentral.com was acquired by Vivendi Universal and renamed Flipside.com.

He then worked at NVFS (`http://www.nvfs.org`) for the Survivors' Fund Project as the Finance and Administration manager supporting the day-to-day operations of the fund and providing technology direction and support. As the Survivors' Fund Project was coming to a close, Tracy moved to Santa Cruz, CA, to become the Technology Director for Quiddities Dev, Inc. (`http://www.quiddities.com`), a web development company based in Santa Cruz. It was at Quiddities that Tracy was introduced to Drupal by one of his co-workers (thanks Rob). Drupal made sense to Tracy, and after the initial learning curve, he embraced Drupal and never looked back. While in Santa Cruz, he became actively involved in the Bay Area Drupal Users Group (BDUG), and the local developer community. Tracy has had the opportunity to work on a range of Drupal sites from small brochure websites to customized e-commerce systems communicating with backend accounting systems.

In 2008, Tracy left Quiddities to start Alpha Geek Tech, LLC, a web development and technology company. Realizing that he had more to learn, Tracy joined the Phase 2 Technology (`http://www.phase2technology.com`) team as a Web Developer in Alexandria, VA.

Acknowledgement

This project has been both a rewarding and learning experience. It could not have been completed without the support of my family, friends, and co-workers. Thanks go to Gibbie and Gary, Gil and Chuck, Pop and Shirley for their constant support and encouragement throughout my life. I appreciate everyone who had the patience to put up with my constantly changing schedule. I am fortunate to have worked with some amazing people over the years and thankful that I have had an opportunity to learn from each of them. I also want to specially thank two of my professors, Betsy Nunn (Data Processing, Arlington County) and Dr. Anne Olsen (CIS, Wingate University) who pushed my learning beyond the standard curriculum.

Finally, each and every page of this book was written with the memory of my mom looking over my shoulder and saying "You can do anything you set your mind to".

It was not until this book was complete, that I realized she was right. Thanks Mom!

About the Reviewers

Dave Poon is a web developer and designer based in Sydney. He started his career as a freelance graphic and web designer in 1998 and worked with web development agencies and medium size enterprises. After graduating from Central Queensland University with a degree in Multimedia Studies and Master degree in IT, he began his love affair with Drupal, and worked for a variety of companies using Drupal.

Currently, Dave is the director of Erlango (http://www.erlango.com), a web product development startup, located in Sydney & Hong Kong, which uses Drupal as a framework to create web products and customized CMS.

He is also the author of Drupal 7 CCK, which is published by Packt Publishing.

I would like to thank my girlfriend, Rita for her endless patience and support. Without her, what I do would be meaningless. Also, I would like to thank my father for his continued encouragement.

Floris van Woudenberg is a Dutch web designer (http://www.flodo.nl). Floris was born and raised in the neighborhood of Utrecht and has been involved with computers since the very first 'home computers' arrived in our homes. Now at the age of 40, he is closely following developments in multimedia and web designing. From his home in Barneveld, Floris is active in developing custom websites for small and medium sized companies. In the past two years, he committed himself as a professional and as a Christian, to providing web solutions for churches throughout the Netherlands.

Due to their flexibility, scalability, and infinite possibilities, Drupal and OpenAtrium have proven to provide the best solutions for this particular group. At the moment, Floris is engaged in using Drupal exclusively so that only projects built in Drupal are being delivered.

I want to give Jesus all credits for my current activities. If He had not intervened in my life, I now would not be where I am nor would I have been able to do what I do. He literally saved me from the edge of life and has provided me with a family, a company, and a vision!

www.PacktPub.com

Support files, eBooks, discount offers, and more

You might want to visit www.PacktPub.com for support files and downloads related to your book.

Did you know that Packt offers e-book versions of every book published with PDF and e-Pub files available? You can upgrade to the e-book version at www.PacktPub.com and as a print book customer, you are entitled to a discount on the e-book copy. Get in touch with us at service@packtpub.com for more details.

At www.PacktPub.com, you can also read a collection of free technical articles, sign up for a range of free newsletters, and receive exclusive discounts and offers on Packt books and e-books.

http://PacktLib.PacktPub.com

Do you need instant solutions to your IT questions? PacktLib is Packt's online digital book library. Here, you can access, read, and search across Packt's entire library of books.

Why Subscribe?

- Fully searchable across every book published by Packt
- Copy and paste, print, and bookmark content
- On demand and accessible through web browser

Free Access for Packt account holders

If you have an account with Packt at www.PacktPub.com, you can use this to access PacktLib today and view nine entirely free books. Simply use your login credentials for immediate access.

Table of Contents

Preface

This book will walk through all the steps required for setting up a basic intranet built on Open Atrium. We review real world examples and provide resources for additional information along the way. Each chapter will address a specific section or feature of Open Atrium and will include information on how you can implement that piece in your own intranet. While this book will cover setting up and configuring Open Atrium, it will not cover developing your own features.

What this book covers

Chapter 1, Overview of Open Atrium, covers what Drupal is and how Open Atrium works with Drupal to provide a foundation for building your intranet. It will provide an overview of the intranet features included with Open Atrium and will discuss what types of entities can benefit from using Open Atrium.

Chapter 2, Setting up a Web Server, looks at the different options for setting up a web server to install Open Atrium. These options include setting up a web server locally on your computer or hosting your website with a web hosting provider. If you already have a web server set up, then you should skip ahead to *Chapter 3, Installation.*

Chapter 3, Installation, provides examples and go through the Open Atrium installation one step at a time. We will start by creating a database, downloading Open Atrium, and finally installing and configuring Open Atrium.

Chapter 4, User Administration, walks through the process of setting up new users, creating accounts, and managing roles. In addition, we will look at the member directory, and setting up user profiles, including how to upload a users avatar or picture.

Chapter 5, Dashboard, provides an explanation of one of the key components of Open Atrium. In this chapter, we will look at creating separate dashboards or home pages for each of your departments or groups. The dashboard allows recent activity items, events, and other items, including blog posts to be brought forward to a central point for each department.

Chapter 6, Groups, provides information about groups, which are individual areas of your site that can be created for your workgroups or departments. Each group can be set to either private or public groups with members. Private groups only expose content to the individual members of that group, while public groups expose any content created by member to all users of an organization.

Chapter 7, Document Library, looks at creating an employee manual that contains several sections. The Document Library feature allows us to maintain a hierarchy of documents, so that items, such as Manuals can be organized and ordered in a manner that makes sense for your organization.

Chapter 8, Blogs, explains another great feature of Open Atrium, which includes a function for blogging. This allows your users to write blog posts that can include references to other items in Open Atrium, including documents, events, or cases. Examples will be provided for creating and editing a blog post and referencing other areas of our site.

Chapter 9, Case Tracker, looks at the Case Tracker feature in Open Atrium. The Case Tracker is versatile in that it can be used as an issue tracker, suggestion box, or a place to submit questions. The Case Tracker divides types of cases up by project and each case can have a priority, status, and case type. The Case Tracker feature assigns a number to each case and maintains a history of commenting and status changes along the way.

Chapter 10, Calendar, provides the necessary information about using the calendar feature in Open Atrium. The calendar feature provides a way to create company events and pull in calendar items from iCal feeds, which are items from an external calendar. An example of an iCal feed would be a list of holidays. Once this feed is pulled in then all the holidays will be listed on your calendar. In this chapter, we will walk through the examples of creating new events and pulling an external calendar.

Chapter 11, Customization, guides you through the process of customizing your Open Atrium. For the most part, Open Atrium will serve your needs with the basic installation. However, there may be times where you want to tweak some of the settings either to match your company's terminology, or change how or what is displayed to the user. This chapter goes through the steps required to alter the Case Tracker types, statuses, and priorities. We will look at customizing Open Atrium views to customize specific items. Lastly, we will look at how to customize the site information, including the site name and footer.

Chapter 12, Open Atrium and Drupal Maintenance, explains the ways by which we can keep our website stable and running. This chapter provides the necessary tools you need to keep your site healthy and running. We will discuss the following:

- Routine maintenance activities
- Performance and caching
- Applying site updates

This chapter will teach you how to maintain your site and review reports to ensure that any questionable issues are addressed prior to it becoming a problem.

Appendix A, Resources, provides additional links on topics discussed through out the book to serve as a reference point for additional information. In this section, we will cover a number of links and documents on the `Drupal.org` site that are helpful for understanding more how Drupal works.

Appendix B, Features & Theming, goes over a key module of Open Atrium named **Features**. Features allow custom snippets of code to be shared among the community, so that we don't have to reinvent the wheel each time we want to add a new feature to our site. Here we introduce you to features and then provide references to find out more information about consuming and developing features for your site. We may also want to customize our sites look and feel and will provide information on where to go to create a new "theme" for our site.

What you need for this book

For this book, you will need access to the internet. Links will be provided if you are setting up your own web server on where to go to download the web server software and the Open Atrium distribution. All of the software required to follow along and install Open Atrium is considered open source and available as free downloads. You will also need a web browser to follow the examples. If you are setting a web server or hosting your site with a web hosting provider, you will want to review the system requirements at the beginning of *Chapter 2*.

Who this book is for

This book is intended for beginners to intermediate computer users who have not worked with Drupal before or want to expand their Drupal knowledge by installing Open Atrium. If you want to learn how to quickly set up an intranet to improve your organization's communication and workflow, then this book is for you.

Conventions

In this book, you will find a number of styles of text that distinguish between different kinds of information. Here are some examples of these styles, and an explanation of their meaning.

Code words in text are shown as follows: "The first two lines in the preceding example copy the default settings file for your site to settings.php for use by Drupal using the cp (copy) command."

Any command-line input or output is written as follows:

```
cd /Applications/MAMP/htdocs <enter>
cp ./sites/default/default.settings.php ./sites/default/settings.php
<enter>
chmod 777 ./sites/default/settings.php <enter>
    chmod 777 ./sites/default <enter>
```

New terms and **important words** are shown in bold. Words that you see on the screen, in menus or dialog boxes for example, appear in the text like this: " Once we have filled out the database name and clicked on **Create**, a message will be displayed under the navigation for phpMyAdmin that says **Database openatrium has been created**."

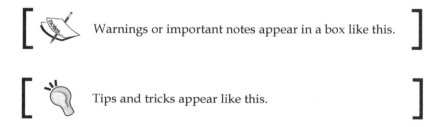

Warnings or important notes appear in a box like this.

Tips and tricks appear like this.

Reader feedback

Feedback from our readers is always welcome. Let us know what you think about this book—what you liked or may have disliked. Reader feedback is important for us to develop titles that you really get the most out of.

To send us general feedback, simply send an e-mail to feedback@packtpub.com, and mention the book title via the subject of your message.

If there is a book that you need and would like to see us publish, please send us a note in the **SUGGEST A TITLE** form on www.packtpub.com or e-mail suggest@packtpub.com.

If there is a topic that you have expertise in and you are interested in either writing or contributing to a book, see our author guide on www.packtpub.com/authors.

Customer support

Now that you are the proud owner of a Packt book, we have a number of things to help you to get the most from your purchase.

Errata

Although we have taken every care to ensure the accuracy of our content, mistakes do happen. If you find a mistake in one of our books—maybe a mistake in the text or the code—we would be grateful if you would report this to us. By doing so, you can save other readers from frustration and help us improve subsequent versions of this book. If you find any errata, please report them by visiting http://www.packtpub.com/support, selecting your book, clicking on the **errata submission form** link, and entering the details of your errata. Once your errata are verified, your submission will be accepted and the errata will be uploaded on our website, or added to any list of existing errata, under the Errata section of that title. Any existing errata can be viewed by selecting your title from http://www.packtpub.com/support.

Piracy

Piracy of copyright material on the Internet is an ongoing problem across all media. At Packt, we take the protection of our copyright and licenses very seriously. If you come across any illegal copies of our works, in any form, on the Internet, please provide us with the location address or website name immediately so that we can pursue a remedy.

Please contact us at copyright@packtpub.com with a link to the suspected pirated material.

We appreciate your help in protecting our authors, and our ability to bring you valuable content.

Questions

You can contact us at questions@packtpub.com if you are having a problem with any aspect of the book, and we will do our best to address it.

1
Overview of Open Atrium

This book is designed to help you become familiar with Open Atrium and Drupal and how the two work together to create a very simple and customizable intranet. Throughout the book, we will use a fictitious company called ACME Inc., to follow as we walk through each example and demonstrate real world functionality. I encourage you to follow along with the examples in each chapter to enrich your experience and learning. Each chapter will be filled with screenshots and how-to's and will provide the building blocks necessary to guide you as you build your intranet using Open Atrium.

In this chapter, we will cover the following three topics:

- What is Drupal?
- What is Open Atrium?
- Who should use Open Atrium?

What is Drupal?

Drupal (`http://drupal.org`) is an open source software program that allows individuals or organizations to easily publish content. Open source software is software that is freely available and created and improved by the community. Drupal can be considered a content management framework that provides a foundation for building a simple or a complex system integrated with custom functionality.

Drupal provides a core set of plugins called modules which provide the basic functions of a content management system including the following:

- User authentication
- Content publishing
- Blog
- Poll
- Statistics and logging
- File uploading

Drupal can be installed by downloading the core package directly from the drupal website (D.O.) or you can add additional functionality right away by downloading and using an installation profile (`http://drupal.org/project/installation+profiles`). An installation profile provides a set of ready made add-on modules and customizations that work along side of the Drupal core modules to provide additional functionality. There are many installation profiles available for Drupal, including profiles for the following:

- Conference organizing
- Education
- Churches
- Wikis
- Project management
- Intranets

For more information about Drupal, you can go to the Drupal website at `http://drupal.org` , also referred to as the "D.O.". The following screenshot is an example of what you will find when you visit the Drupal website:

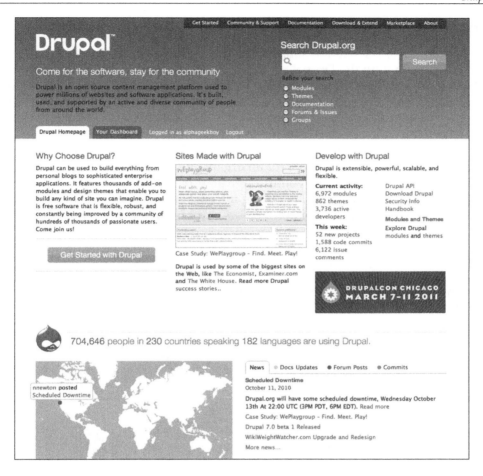

We will be working with the Open Atrium (`http://openatrium.org`) installation profile originally created by Development Seed (`http://developmentseed.org`), an online communications consultancy based in Washington, DC.

What is Open Atrium?

Open Atrium is a specialized installation of Drupal that adds on modules and incorporates them with the Drupal core to provide intranet functionality. It is an installation profile (http://drupal.org/project/installation+profiles) for Drupal. As with all installation profiles, it includes the Drupal core files along with all the customizations and modules used by Development Seed and the open source community to create a basic intranet. Installation profiles are also referred to as Drupal distributions because they include the core Drupal files with the distribution. An intranet can be defined as a tool for an organization to communicate and share information. This book will take you through step-by-step on how to install, setup, and use Open Atrium. To create a working intranet on top of Drupal without an installation profile would require many hours of additional programming, and integration of available modules. The installation profile reduces the amount of time it takes to get up and running by eliminating the need for additional programming or installing extra modules on top of Drupal to create a working intranet.

The following screenshot shows how the Open Atrium home page looks at http://openatrium.com:

Intranet in a box

Open Atrium comes built-in with basic intranet features to be used as a tool for groups to share information. In this installation there is a module called team spaces, which provides mini sites within your installation for your departments or workgroups. You are not limited to the features included with the base installation. Because Open Atrium is open source, features that are developed for Open Atrium by other organizations can be made available as an easy plugin to install on your own site. You can also develop your own set of features and integrate them with Open Atrium.

Team spaces

At the core of Open Atrium is a concept called **group** or **team spaces**. This feature allows individual projects or departments to set up their own unique space which includes all of the features of Open Atrium. Each group administrator can set the visibility of their group space to either private or public. When visibility is set to public, everyone in the organization can view and contribute to the groups team space. However, if the visibility is set to private, then only group members of that team space can contribute and view content. It is likely that your intranet will include a mix of private and public spaces depending on the workgroup or teams goals. For example, a Human Resources (HR) department may have both a private space for policy discussion and a public space for publishing general HR information and soliciting feedback.

Each team space incorporates the following features of Open Atrium:

- Blog
- Calendar
- Group dashboard
- Documents
- Shoutbox
- Case tracker

Blogs

A blog can exist in many forms. For the most part, a blog is interactive and allows for commenting on specific blog topics. A member of a department can create a blog entry on a specific topic and allow other members to become involved in the conversation by commenting. When the blog is set up in Open Atrium, the creator has the chance to mark the blog private or public. If the blog is public, then the blog writer will have the option to post their blog entry to their particular department, or post the entry to the whole organization. File attachments can be included with each blog entry or comment. Each blog author or commenter has granular control of which members of the organization are notified of the interaction. In *Chapter 8*, we will walk through setting up a blog for the Human Resources (HR) department of ACME Inc.

The following screenshot shows an example of a blog summary page for the HR department at ACME Inc:

Calendar

The calendar feature allow you to post events for single day events with a start and end time or events spanning across multiple days. The calendar feature is rich in functionality and allows us to pull in additional iCalendar (iCal) feeds from other calendars. An iCal feed provides basic information about each event including date, time, and description, which is based on a standard format for calendar data exchange. It allows you to pull in feeds published by other organizations or companies. You can set up your calendar to pull in feeds from Google Calendars, holiday calendars, and any calendar that is published using the iCal standard. You can add as many calendar feeds as you like and have them appear on your groups calendar.

The following screenshot shows an example calendar for the HR department with a manual event for on the HR Winter Festival on February 11, 2011:

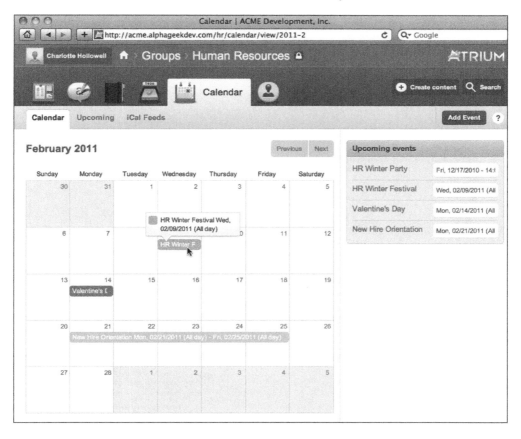

Group dashboard

The group dashboard is available for all of the groups that you belong to and provides an overview of the activity for your group. There is also a site dashboard when you first login that shows information pertaining to any of the public groups and private groups that you may belong to. It is the first page by default that is shown when you navigate to your group. The dashboard consists of mini widgets that include calendar entries, blog entries, files, and comments. The layout, as well as what appears on the dashboard page, is fully customizable through the settings option. You can arrange items in a way that makes sense for your group or department.

The following screenshot shows the group dashboard for the HR department at ACME Inc:

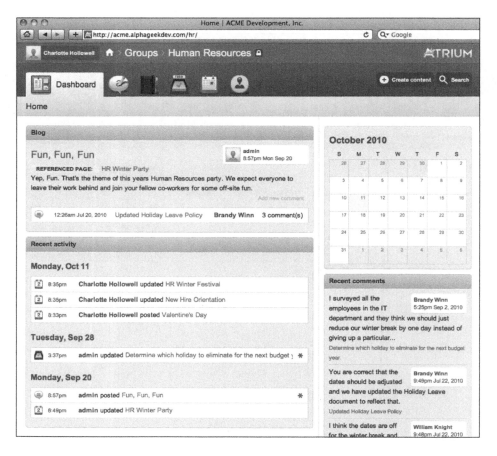

Document library

The document section of Open Atrium is flexible and allows us to create one or more **handbooks**, also referred to as a **notebook**. A handbook is a collection of documents with a hierarchy that can be used within your department. Examples of handbooks could include:

- Manuals
- Forms
- Policy and procedures
- Issues
- Images and branding
- Form letters

The document section allows us to collaborate on documents as well as store and compare revisions to documents. You can also attach files and print out a final version of the handbook once all changes are complete. Each handbook consists of a main page and subsequent child pages. This allows the department to store and organize information in a manner that makes sense to them. Child pages can be rearranged, so that the final order of the documents can be completed at a later time. You can even attach different types of files including PDFs, documents, and images.

The following screenshot shows the notebook section of the HR's department team space:

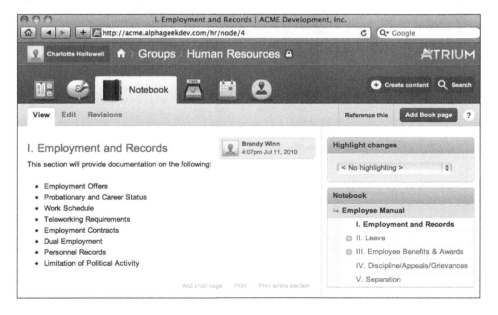

Shoutbox

The Shoutbox feature of Open Atrium allows you to share short messages with people in your group or organization depending on your settings. It is similar to Twitter (`http://twitter.com`) where you can leave short messages to be displayed within the Shoutbox. However, it differs from Twitter in that the Shoutbox is only available to view for members of your group space. By typing in the Shoutbox area, you can share messages, links, and any other information necessary. These messages and links will be displayed in a chronological order on the Shoutbox page. Depending upon your configuration you can also choose to have them show up on the dashboard page as well.

The Shoutbox is a pop-up window feature where you can review the most recent shouts or type a new shout. There is also a link to the *Full view* on the bottom of the pop-up to go to the main Shoutbox page. The Shoutbox page also contains a search box to allow us to search for a specific piece of information. We can type a search term and then all the related Shoutbox messages will be retrieved. Group members' pictures or avatars are also listed on this page by default.

The following screenshot shows an example Shoutbox page with a few messages created by ACME's HR department:

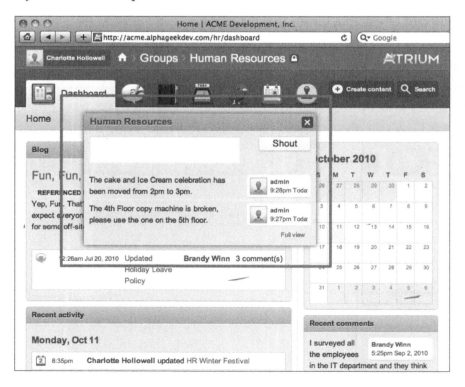

Case Tracker

The **Case Tracker** feature of Open Atrium provides a full ticketing system that your department can use to create projects, track bugs, and maintain to do lists. The system allows us to create one or more projects and add issues or items to each one. We can then assign each item to a particular person in our group and provide a priority, status, and request type. This can be used to track ongoing status of a project and is flexible enough to track bugs within a particular project. The **Case Tracker** screen provides a summary of cases on the first tab and provides additional tabs to view your own cases, department wide projects, and any archived projects.

A search filter is exposed on the right-hand side of the screen that allows the searching of cases by the assignee, project, priority, or status.

The following screenshot shows an example Case Tracker screen with three open cases from two different projects within ACME's HR department:

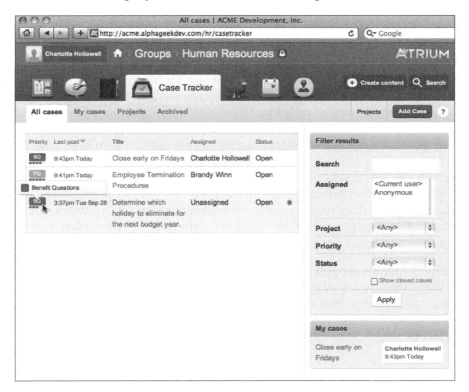

Each open case is listed on a separate row. The first column contains a colored box with an abbreviation for the project that a particular case belongs to. We can see in the screenshot that as you hover over one of these boxes, the full project name is listed.

Summary of features

Open Atrium seamlessly integrates the following features together:

- Blogs
- Calendar
- Dashboard (group and individual)
- Wiki (document library/notebook)
- Shoutbox
- Bug/Issue system (case tracker)

The beauty of Open Atrium is that all of these features are available immediately after the initial installation. Even if you have never heard of Drupal or Open Atrium, after reading this book you will be able to install, configure, and immediately use Open Atrium for your organization or department.

Who should use Open Atrium?

Open Atrium can be used by any organization and for any site that requires intranet like functionality. There are many project management and intranet applications available as a software service or for purchase. As Open Atrium is open source, you can be assured that it is freely available for immediate download and installation. If your company is already using Drupal, then Open Atrium would be a perfect addition to your companies network of sites. If you don't have Drupal experience in-house, you can use this book as a guide to walk through each step of setting up your intranet. Open Atrium is a great candidate for sites or teams that need project management, document sharing, and issue tracking. It can be used as a communication tool to provide your resources with timely information and can improve the workflow of your organization.

Because Open Atrium is open source and built on top of the Drupal platform, you will find that there are a vast number of resources available. The Open Atrium distribution and is supported by a community site located at `http://community.openatrium.com`. This site provides resources for both end-users and developers.

Summary

In this chapter, we started out talking about what Drupal is and what it includes. At its core, Drupal includes user authentication, content publishing, statistics and logging, and blog functionality. Drupal is an open source content management framework that can be downloaded for free from the Drupal website. We covered installation profiles that are prepackaged Drupal distributions that can be used to install Drupal for specific applications, including the following:

- Conference organizing
- Education sites
- Church sites
- Intranets

The next section talked about Open Atrium and the rich features that are included with the distribution. Open Atrium provides departments and organizations the ability to create team spaces for individual work groups and includes the following features:

- Blog
- Calendar
- Group dashboard
- Document library
- Shoutbox
- Case tracker

We then covered who should use Open Atrium and how it can easily be implemented for any team or working group for project management and communications within each group.

In the following chapter, we will learn how to create the foundation to install Open Atrium, by learning how to setup a web server and where we can go for more information for hosting our Open Atrium website.

2
Setting up a Web Server

In this chapter, we will walk through the steps necessary to install and configure a local hosted web server on your computer. We will go through the steps necessary to set up a web server on both the Mac and Windows environment. If you want to set up your web server in a Linux environment information will be provided for additional resources. If you already have a web server set up and available to use then you skip ahead to *Chapter 3, Installation.* If you are not comfortable setting up your own web server, then follow the instructions on setting up a hosted server or have someone set one up for you and then continue to *Chapter 3* In this chapter, we will build the foundation for your Open Atrium installation and will cover the following topics:

- System requirements
- Setting up a local web server
- Setting up a hosted web server

With each step of the web server installation, a screenshot will be provided with detailed instructions on what options to select during the installation. Once we've completed this section we will have a working web server to install Open Atrium on.

System requirements

To install Open Atrium, you will need a web server capable of rendering PHP pages and a database server.

Web server

When it comes to selecting a web server there are primarily two options for running Open Atrium and Drupal, which are as follows:

- Apache
- Microsoft IIS

Apache is by far the most popular and easiest to configure for Open Atrium. The Open Atrium distribution has been developed and successfully tested on the Apache platform. The examples in this book will use the Apache web server.

For Apache the requirements are as follows:

- PHP 5.2
- PHP GD extension
- 64MB memory limit
- MySQL 5
- Apache mod_rewrite module for clean URLs

 For PHP it is best to use a 5.2.x version as there are some known issues with incompatibilities between some Drupal modules and PHP 5.3.

For MySQL, you should use Version 5.0.41 or higher as there have been known incompatibilities with the "Recent Activity" listing feature in Open Atrium.

Browsers

Open Atrium supports most of the major standards-compliant browsers and has been tested on the following clients:

- Firefox 2+
- Safari 3+
- Internet Explorer 7+

Internet Explorer 6 or clients with JavaScript disabled are not supported.

 You can read more about the system requirements for Drupal and Open Atrium at the following websites:

http://drupal.org/requirements

http://openatrium.com/documentation/requirements

Web server platform

For setting up our web server we have the following two methods available to us:

- Hosted web server
- Local web server

Using a hosted server from a web host provider is the easiest and best route to follow. If you are adventurous and want to setup Open Atrium on your own computer, then you should follow the local web server instructions. A hosted server will be the easiest to set up because we do not have to deal with configuring a local machine to run the LAMP stack (Linux, Apache, MySQL, and PHP). However, you will have more control over your web server if it is locally hosted and won't need to be connected to the internet to run Open Atrium.

Hosted web server

If you don't already have a web hosting provider you can perform a search for "web hosting providers". Once you've selected a hosting company make sure that they provide access to the command line/SSH access and access to your php.ini file. Also, make sure that the web hosting provider can meet the system requirements in the first part of this chapter. The basic steps for setting up a web host are as follows:

1. Select a web host provider.
2. Select a domain name.
3. Sign up with a web host provider.
4. Review any additional setup instructions sent to you by your web hosting provider.

Once we have completed the preceding steps, you should be able to access the new site at the domain name you provided and view the web server default page. You may have to wait a few hours for your site to be set up.

Local web server

You have several options for installing a local web server depending on the type of computer you are using. This book will include instructions for setting up a web server on a Mac and a Windows PC. Mac users will want to install **MAMP (Mac, Apache, MySQL, PHP)** and Windows users will want to install **WAMP (Windows, Apache, MySQL, PHP)**.

If you are on a Linux based system and want to learn how to install a web server there are several resources available on the web including the following:

`http://webdesign.about.com/cs/apache/a/aainstallapache.htm`

`http://www.lamphowto.com/`

Mac installation—MAMP setup

In this section, we will go over the steps necessary to install a web server on a Mac computer. If you are using a windows system, then you should skip ahead to the *Windows Installation — WAMP setup* section.

To set up a web server on the Mac we will go through the following steps:

1. Download.
2. License agreement.
3. Copy to applications folder.
4. Change the default folder.
5. Open start page.

Step 1: Download

To download the code for the MAMP server for Mac, we can go to `http://mamp.info/en/index.html` and click on the **Download now** link for the **MAMP: One-click solution for setting up your personal web server**. The following screenshot shows an example of the MAMP website and which button to click:

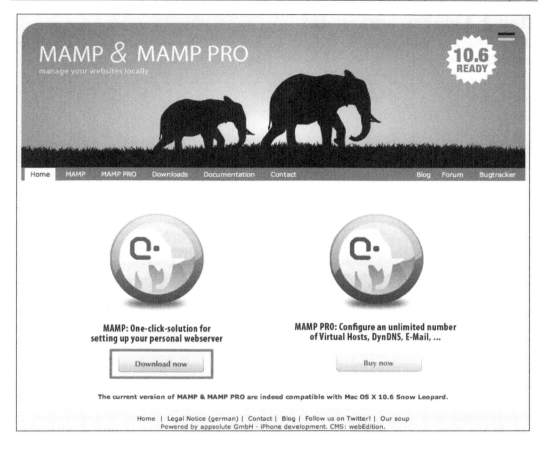

It is a large download (156Mb), so it may take a few minutes to download. Once the download is complete locate the file in Finder. The file should be in your downloads folder and named something like the following:

MAMP_MAMP_PRO_1.8.4.dmg.zip

Double-click the file to extract the disk image. You should now see another file named the same without the .zip extension. Double-click this file to launch the installer.

Step 2: License agreement

Click on **Agree** on the following screen to accept the license agreement and begin the installation:

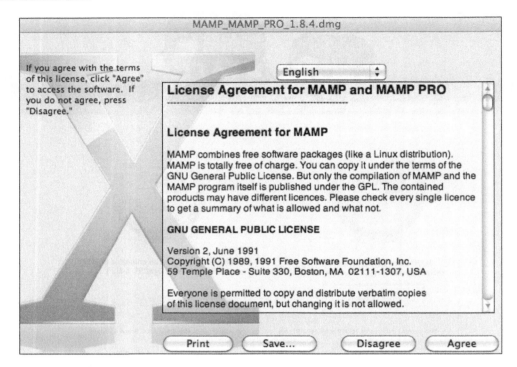

Step 3: Copy to applications folder

The next screen instructs you to copy the MAMP folder into your Applications folder. Click on the **MAMP** folder on the left and drag and drop it into the **Applications** folder at the top as shown in the following screenshot:

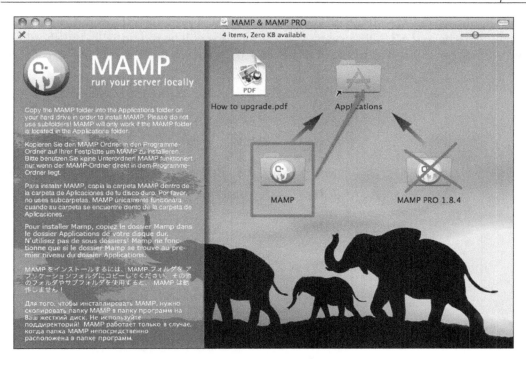

Step 4: Start MAMP

Go to your `Applications` folder and locate the `MAMP` folder. Double-click on the `MAMP.app` file that is shown in the following screenshot:

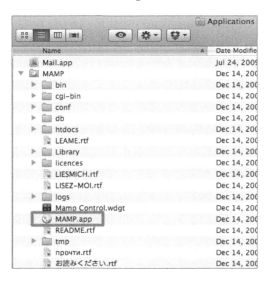

You should see the MAMP control window which will provide a status indicator for the Apache and MySQL servers. The **Status** icons will be red initially, but should switch to green as soon as the servers are started, as shown in the following screenshot:

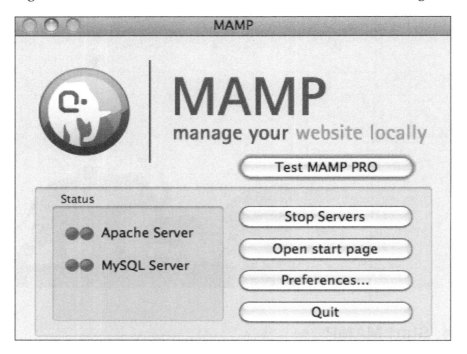

Once the servers are started, your default browser should automatically open to the default web server page. If it does not, you can click on **Open start page** on the MAMP control panel. The following is an example of the default web server page:

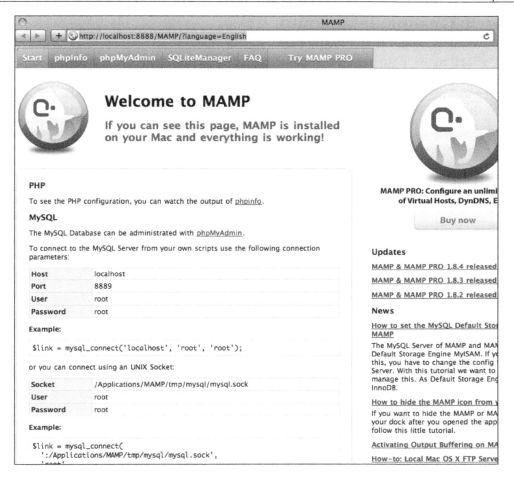

Once we see this page, then we know that we have installed everything correctly.

Step 5: Change default port

To make things easier we will want to change the default port to 80 for our localhost. This will allow us to go to `http://localhost` URL in our browser instead of having add on the port number to the end of the URL (`http://localhost:8889`). Click on **Preferences** on the MAMP control panel and then click on the **Ports** tab. The following screenshot shows the *port configuration* after we have set them to the default:

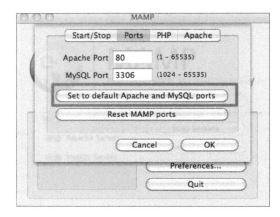

Click on **Set to default Apache and MySQL ports** and then click on **OK**. A prompt will ask for the administrator password for the computer to save the settings. The web server will restart and the status lights should return to green.

Step 6: Open start page

We should then be able to click on the **Open start page** in the MAMP control panel and see the start page. Congratulations we have now successfully installed a web server on a MAC including Apache, MySQL, and PHP.

More Information:
MAMP install instructions: `http://www.sawmac.com/mamp/`
MAMP documentation: `http://mamp.info/en/documentation/index.html`

Windows installation—WAMP setup

Carry out the following steps to set up a web server on Windows:

Step 1: Download WAMP

Go to `http://www.wampserver.com/en` and click on the link **Download the latest release of Wampserver 2**, as shown in the following screenshot:

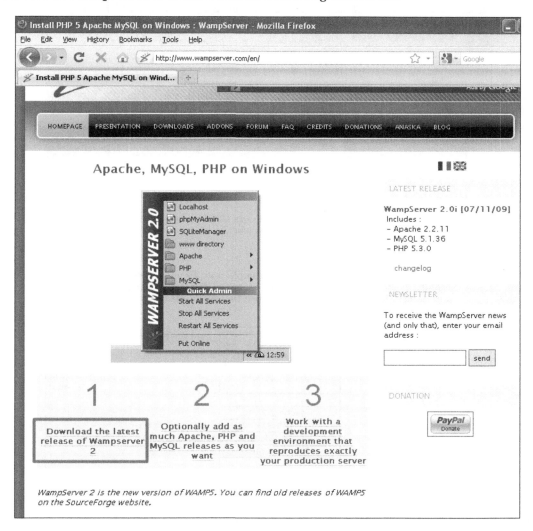

On the next page you will see an option to **DOWNLOAD WampServer 2.0i**. Click on that link as indicated in the following screenshot:

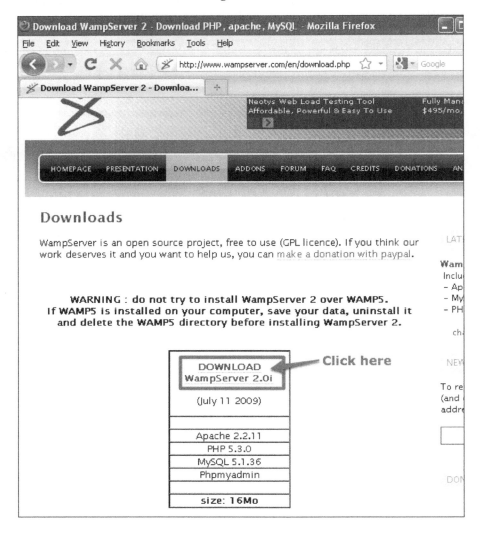

You should then see an option to **save this file**. Click on **Save File**. Locate the downloaded file, which should be named something like `WampServer2.0i.exe`, and double-click on it to start the WAMP installation.

Step 2: Welcome screen

The welcome screen should appear, as shown in the following screenshot:

Click on **Next** to continue.

Step 3: License agreement

Click on the option for **I accept the agreement** and then click on **Next** to continue, as shown in the following screenshot:

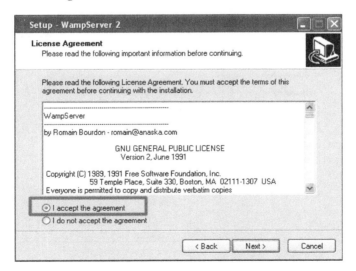

Step 4: Destination location

Click on **Next** to accept the default destination, which should be `c:\wamp`, as shown in the following screenshot:

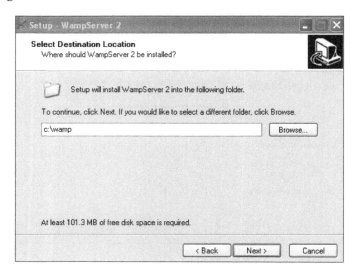

Step 5: Select additional tasks

You can optionally create a quick launch icon and a desktop icon by checking the checkbox next to each item. Then click on **Next** as shown in the following screenshot:

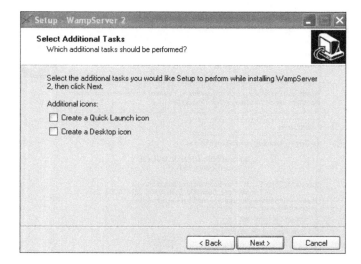

Step 6: Install

Click on **Install** to begin the WAMP installation as seen in the following screenshot:

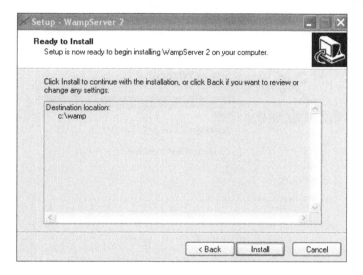

Step 7: PHP mail parameters

For now, you can accept the default values for SMTP and Email. Or we can fill in a SMTP host and our own e-mail address to send e-mails out from our own address.

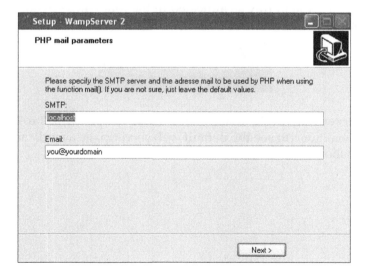

Step 8: Setup complete

On this screen you can click on **Finish** to finish the installation and launch your WAMP Server, as depicted in the following screenshot:

Step 9: Start web server

The web server should load and show up as a tiny icon in your system tray. If it does not show up in your system tray as indicated in the following screenshot, you can go to **Start | Programs | WampServer | Start WampServer**:

Once the web server starts, you should then be able to open your browser and go to `http://localhost` to see the default web server page as indicated in the following screenshot:

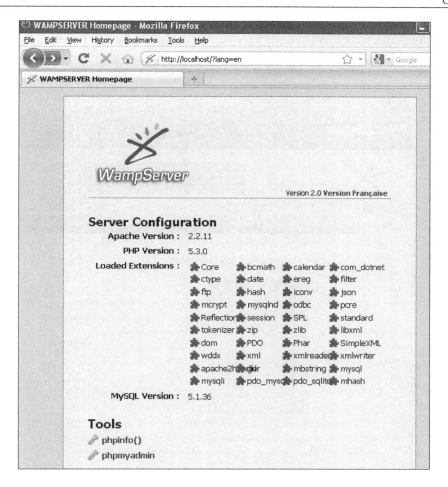

Installing PHP 5.2.11

The WAMP server comes packaged with PHP 5.3 by default and at the time of this printing there are some known incompatibilities with PHP 5.3, Open Atrium, and Drupal. To fix this issue we will walk through the steps necessary to install PHP 5.2.11.

To install PHP 5.2.x we can go back to the http://www.wampserver.com/en/ web page and click on number **2** to **Optionally add as much Apache, PHP and MySQL releases as you want**. The next screenshot shows where to click:

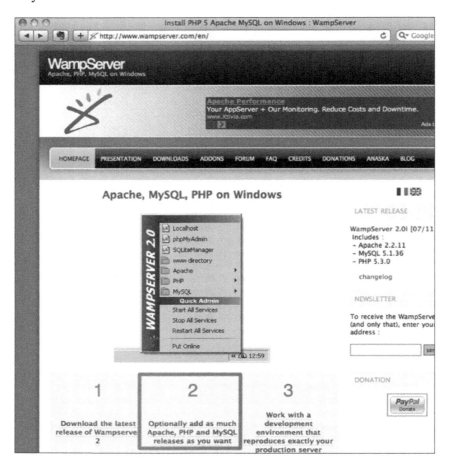

On the next page under **ADDONS,** click on the **PHP** link. Scroll down the page and click on the **PHP 5.2.11** link which will install the latest version of PHP 5.2 that is compatible with Open Atrium and Drupal.

This will launch the PHP 5.2.11 installation. We can accept all the defaults for the installation and click on **Install**. Once the server is installed, you can click on the **Quick Menu** to switch the PHP version to 5.2.11.

The last step we need to is modify the ini settings for PHP to increase the memory limit and maximum execution time. To edit the file we can click on the WAMP menu icon in the system tray and click on php.ini to open the file in Notepad. Search for maximum_execution_time and change the value from 30 to 90. Then search for memory_limit and edit the value for memory limit from 128MB to 256MB.

Congratulations we now have a WAMP Server installed and ready for use.

 You may want to make this your browser's default home page, so that you don't have to keep typing the http://localhost URL every time.

Summary

Congratulations, we now have a working web server installation.

In the previous sections we covered the system requirements for Drupal and Open Atrium, which at a minimum include Apache, PHP 5.2, and MySQL 5.x. We then presented two options for running your server either by hosting it locally on your computer, or by selecting a web hosting provider. The last section then walked through the steps required to set up a local web server on using a MAMP (Mac) web server and WAMP (Windows) web server.

In *Chapter 3, Installation*, we will walk through the steps required to install Open Atrium.

3
Installation

Now that we have a web server set up, we will cover the steps necessary for installing Open Atrium. The first two parts of this chapter will contain information about installation on two different types of environments, Mac (MAMP) and Windows (WAMP). You should follow the sections with the heading for your particular environment. This chapter is divided into the following three parts:

- Part I: Creating a database
- Part II: Drupal and Open Atrium installation
- Part III: Drupal administration

In Part I, we will provide instructions for creating a database to support the Open Atrium installation. If you are using a web host provider for your site, you will need to consult their documentation for creating a database. Then once you have created a database, you can continue on to Part II: Drupal and Open Atrium installation.

There are several ways to install Open Atrium and in Part II we will use the browser based installation for Open Atrium. With each step of the installation, we will provide a screenshot and detailed instructions on what options to select. After completing Part II, you will have a working installation of Open Atrium Distribution.

Part III will present a quick tour of the Drupal administration section of Open Atrium. In this section, we will highlight several Drupal administration functions. Most of Open Atrium can be managed through the Open Atrium interface and we will not have to go into the Drupal administration section that often. However, there will be a few tasks that need to be performed in the Drupal administration section. Part III will provide enough of an overview to feel at ease on any Drupal administration task you may have to perform.

Part 1: Creating a database

The first thing that we need to do before installing Open Atrium is to create a database. This section will walk through the process of creating a database on a Mac (MAMP) and Windows (MAMP) development environment. Each section will contain specific instructions for your environment that you can follow. If you are comfortable with MySQL and the command-line, you can add a database through the command-line. These instructions will walk through how to add a database using a web-based program named phpMyAdmin, which provides a frontend interface to your MySQL server installed with MAMP.

Step 1: Launching phpMyAdmin

Mac (MAMP)

If the MAMP control panel is not already running, we can launch the control panel by opening Finder and going to the Application folder. Double-click on the MAMP icon in the Finder window. The MAMP control panel should launch and a green status indicator should be displayed next to the Apache and MySQL servers. Once the control panel is launched, click on the **Open start page** button to open the web server's default page. After the start page is loaded, we can click on the **phpMyAdmin** link at the top of the page as shown in the following screenshot:

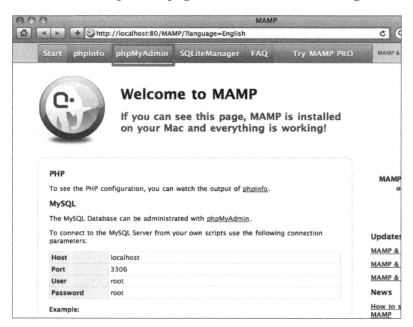

Clicking on this link will load the phpMyAdmin utility where you will create a database. Now you can go to Step 2: creating a database.

Windows (WAMP)

If the WAMP Server is not already running, then launch the WAMP Server by going to **Start | Programs | WampServer | Start WAMPServer**. Now open your browser and go to http://localhost and you should see the WampServer's default page. On this page under **Tools**, you can click on **phpmyadmin** as shown in the following screenshot:

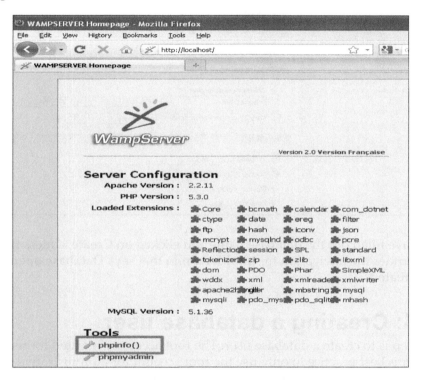

Clicking on this link will load the phpMyAdmin utility where you will create a database. Now you can continue to Step 2: creating a database.

Step 2: Creating a database—Mac (MAMP) and Windows (WAMP)

Steps 2 and 3 are the same for both the MAMP and WAMP environments. Now that we have launched phpMyAdmin, we can create the database that we will use for Open Atrium. On the phpMyAdmin page, we will see a section labeled **MySQL localhost**. In this section, there is a form field named **Create new database**. For the examples in this book, we will use the database named openatrium. The following screenshot shows the phpMyAdmin page with the database name filled in:

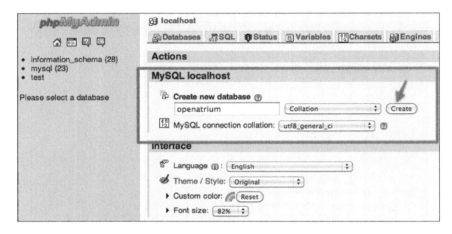

Once we have filled out the database name and clicked on **Create**, a message will be displayed under the navigation for phpMyAdmin that says **Database openatrium has been created**.

Step 3: Creating a database user

The next step is to create a database user. The root account is created for us. However, it is best practice to only use the root account for administrative purposes. In this step, we will set up a user that will only be used by your Open Atrium installation. Click on **Privileges** on the phpMyAdmin navigation and then click on **Add a new User** at the bottom as shown in the following screenshot:

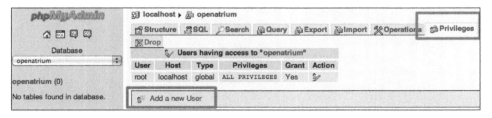

Once on the **Add a new User** screen, fill in the **User name** and **Password** fields with the following:

User name: sql_openatrium

Password: oainstall

Re-type: oainstall

We can use any user name or password. However, the examples in this book will assume that you have used the preceding user name and password. Then at the very bottom of the screen click on **GO**. You can see a screen similar to the following screenshot:

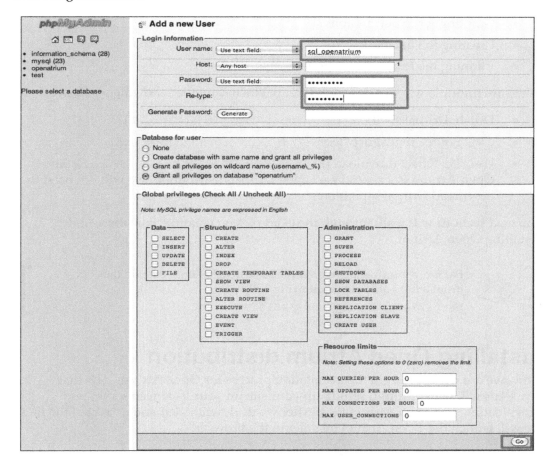

A message should now be displayed at the top of your phpMyAdmin page that says "You have added a new user". Congratulations, we've added our first MySQL user. At this point, we can close the browser and proceed to Part II.

Part II: Drupal and Open Atrium installation

Once you have a web server setup, installing Drupal requires carrying out a set of simple steps which include the following:

- Downloading Drupal
- Granting write permissions
- Creating the database
- Running the installation script

There are multiple ways to download Drupal including the following:

- Drush: Drupal shell (`http://drupal.org/project/drush`)
- CVS: Source repository (`http://drupal.org/handbook/cvs`)
- Website: Direct download (`http://drupal.org/project/drupal`). Since Open Atrium is a special packaged Drupal distribution, we will not need to download Drupal separately.

The next sections will walk through the examples on creating a database and installing Open Atrium.

 For more information refer to the basic installation section in the installation guide at the following URL:
`http://drupal.org/node/251019`

Installing Open Atrium distribution

Now, we are ready to begin the installation process for Open Atrium. The first few steps will walk through setting up your site on your local web server and downloading the Open Atrium files. After we've downloaded and extracted the files, we will launch the Open Atrium installer in the browser.

Step 1: Setting up your site

The first thing we need to do is determine where to place the files that you will download in step 2. This process is slightly different depending on what platform you are on. In this step, there are specific instructions for both the Mac (MAMP) and Windows (WAMP) environments that you can follow depending on your environment.

Mac (MAMP)

Locate in Finder the directory under **Applications | MAMP** named htdocs. This is the directory where you will place the extracted files from step 2. This will be your default website directory. Double-click the htdocs directory to open it in Finder. The path will be /Applications/MAMP/htdocs/.

 You can drag and drop the htdocs directory in Finder under the **Places** section to create a shortcut to this directory.

Windows (WAMP)

For WAMP users, we will need to create a new directory in c:\wamp\www for the Open Atrium installation. The easiest way to do this is to go to the **Start** menu and click on **run**. Then type c:\wamp\www and then click on OK. This is shown in the following screenshot:

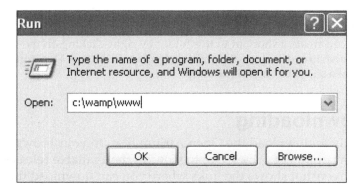

Now click on **File | New | Folder** to create a new folder. For the folder name, we will use OpenAtrium. When you are done, the c:\wamp\www should look like the following screenshot:

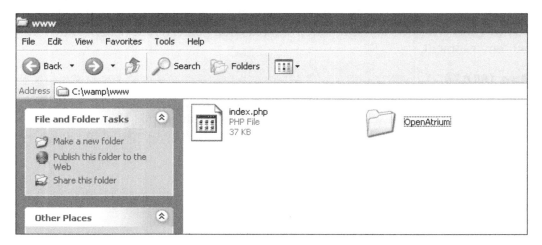

You can close this window and open your browser again and go to http://localhost, or refresh the WampServer's default page if you still have it open. Under the section **Your Projects**, you will now see an **OpenAtrium** project which you can click on to go to the site. At this point, we haven't placed any files in the directory and will only see a blank index page.

> **Tip: Windows (WAMP) Shortcut**
>
> You can create a shortcut to this folder by right-clicking on the **OpenAtrium** directory and then clicking on **Send to | Desktop**. This will create a shortcut on your desktop.

Step 2: Downloading

Now we are ready to download the Open Atrium files. In your browser, go to http://openatrium.com/download to view all the available releases. The following screenshot shows the links where you can download the files depending on your environment:

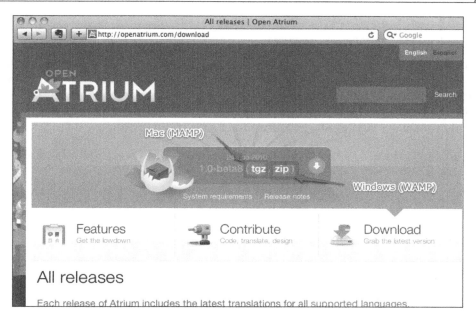

The procedure for downloading and extracting the files vary slightly based on your environment.

Mac (MAMP)

Click on the **tgz** link at the top of the page to begin downloading the Open Atrium distribution. Double-click the **tgz** file to begin the unarchive process. Now we will move the files from this directory to our website directory.

Open a terminal window by double-clicking on the `Terminal.app` in **Applications | Utilities**. The first thing we will do in terminal is change the directory to the extracted directory. We will want to change the last part of the CD command to reflect the actual directory name of our extracted files. In this example, `atrium-1-0` is the directory name.

```
cd ~/Downloads/atrium-1-0 <enter>
mv * /Applications/MAMP/ <enter>
```

We also want to create the default `settings.php` file and set permissions for the installation to work correctly. To do this, type the following lines in the same terminal window:

```
cd /Applications/MAMP/htdocs <enter>
cp ./sites/default/default.settings.php ./sites/default/settings.php
<enter>
```

```
chmod 777 ./sites/default/settings.php <enter>

chmod 777 ./sites/default <enter>
```

The first two lines in the preceding example copy the default settings file for your site to settings.php for use by Drupal using the cp (copy) command. The last two lines change the permissions for the settings.php file and the default directory to be writeable. Once the installation is complete, we will set these permissions back to read-only for security. We can now close the terminal window.

Open the /Applications/MAMP/htdocs/sites/default directory in Finder and we should see the following screen:

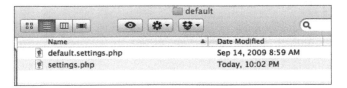

Windows (WAMP)

Click on the **zip** link at the top of the page to begin downloading the Open Atrium distributions. Locate the downloaded ZIP file and right-click on the ZIP file and select **Extract All**. The files will be extracted into a directory with the same name as the file downloaded. The directory will be named based on the release download and will look similar to atrium-1-0.

Next, we need to copy the files extracted to our web root directory (c:\wamp\www). To do this, right-click on the extracted files directory and select **Copy**. Then navigate to c:\wamp\www through explorer and open that directory. Right-click inside this directory and choose **Paste** to copy the Open Atrium files to this directory. Now, we need to create a settings file for the installation. To do this, navigate to the c:\wamp\www\OpenAtrium\sites\default directory through Windows Explorer and right-click on the default.settings.php file and select **Copy**. Then right-click in the folder and choose **Paste**. We should now have the following two files in this folder:

- default.settings.php
- Copy of default.settings.php

Right-click on **Copy of default.settings.php** and select **Rename**. Change the filename to settings.php. When completed, the default directory should look like the following:

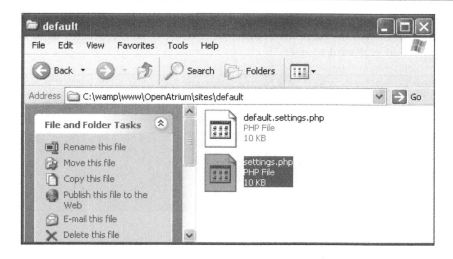

Step 3: Open Atrium browser installation

Both Mac (MAMP) and Windows (WAMP) users will use the same set of instructions for installing Open Atrium through the browser. The complicated part is over as you have a working web server with the Open Atrium files in your web root directory. This step will take us through the Open Atrium installation page by page. Open the browser and go to `http://localhost`. We should see the following page:

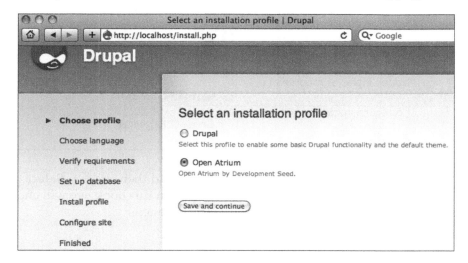

We have two options for the installation and we will want to select the default option of **Open Atrium**. Click on **Save and continue**. The next screen allows us to choose the language that we want to use:

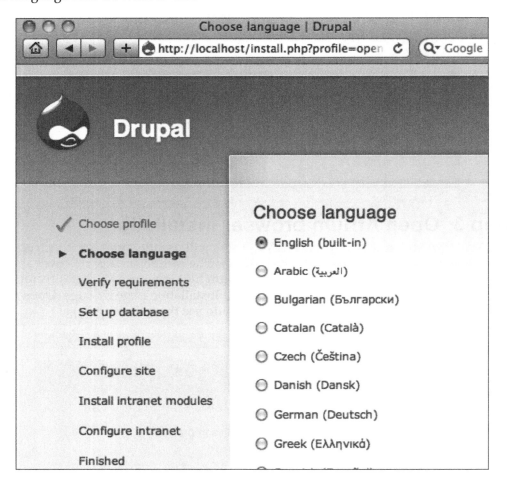

Here we can select the language that we want to use and then click on **Select language** at the bottom of the page. For the examples in this book, we will choose **English**. The next page is the database configuration page:

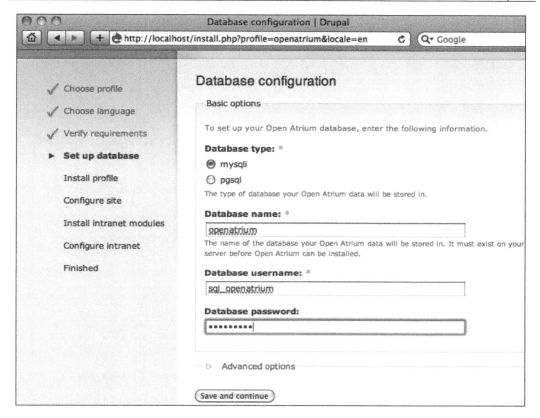

When we set up the database, we created a database name, user name, and password. This is where we input those settings for Open Atrium to set up the database. On this screen, keep the default of **mysqli** for database type and then fill in the following fields:

Database name: openatrium

Database username: sql_openatrium

Database password: oainstall

After clicking on **Save and continue** the database will be created and then we will continue on to the **Configure site** page. There are three sections on this page where we will fill out some basic information about our site. They include the following:

- Site information
- Administrator account
- Server settings

In the **Site information** section, we will fill out the **Site name** and **Site e-mail address** as shown in the following screenshot:

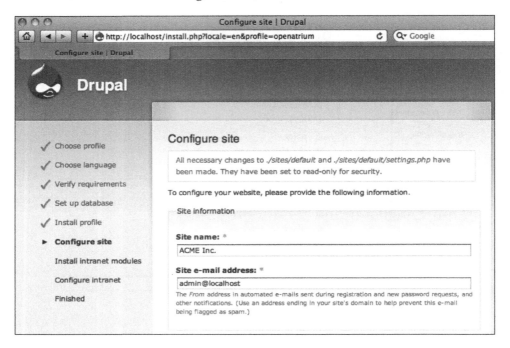

The next part asks for **Administrator account** information which includes our user name, e-mail address, and password as shown in the following screenshot:

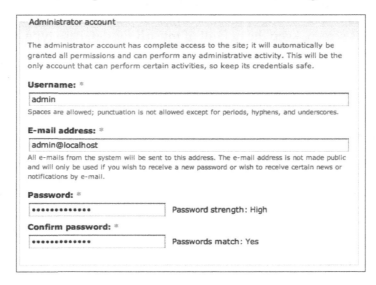

The last step in the installation of Open Atrium asks for some server settings. In this section, we will select our time zone, verify whether clean URLs are enabled, and ensure that updates are checked automatically.

After selecting the **Default time zone** in the drop-down box, you should be able to select the defaults for the rest of the options. You may notice that **Clean URLs** are enabled. Clean URLs allow your site to render URLs without a "?" and instead uses the slash (/) character for separating URL variables.

> In *Chapter 2*, we installed Apache with the defaults which should have had the mod_rewrite module enabled. If for some reason mod_rewrite was not enabled to use clean URLs, you will need to do a search on how to enable mod_rewrite for your environment.

The following screenshot shows what the server settings should look like for our site:

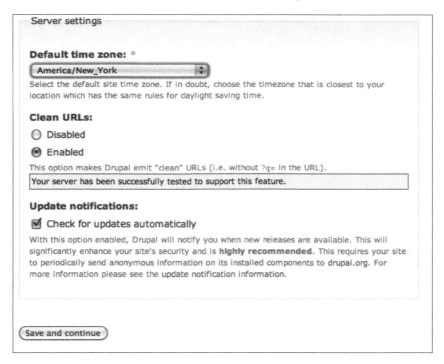

Once we have reviewed the information, we can click on **Save and continue** to finish the installation. The last screen will show that we have completed all the steps to install Open Atrium and will provide a link to visit your new site. The final screen of the installation looks like the following screenshot:

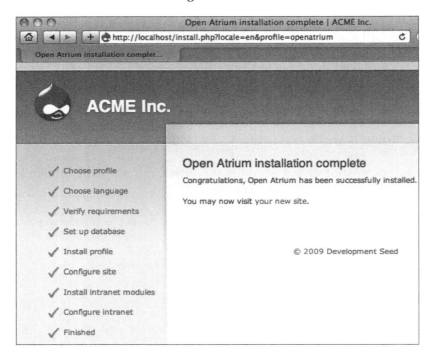

Congratulations, you have successfully installed Open Atrium and now have a working Open Atrium site.

Part III: Drupal administration

There are two main places where configuration and tweaks will take place to maintain our site. The majority of administration tasks will be performed through the Open Atrium interface. However, there will be a few items that we will need to complete behind the scenes in the Drupal admin section. This section will cover the Drupal administration area to provide a quick overview of some of the administrative tasks we may be required to perform in Drupal.

Open Atrium home page

When you first open your site after installation, you should see the Atrium home page. If you closed your browser window after installation go to `http://localhost` and log in using the user name and password that you provided during the installation. Once logged in, we will see the following screen in the left column of the Open Atrium home page:

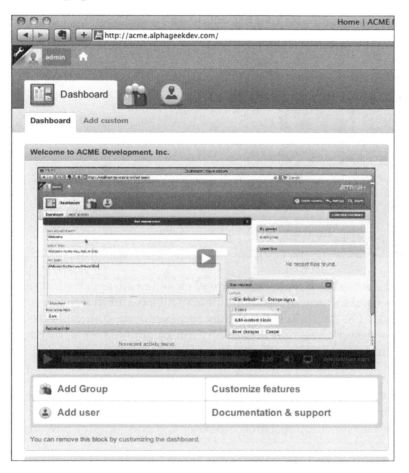

 The middle part of this screenshot will be blurry because there is a video embedded in the page.

On this screen, we can click on the **Play** button to watch the welcome video. For now, we will click on the wrench icon located in the upper left corner of the screen. We will see the wrench anytime we are logged in as a user with administrative privileges. It is our shortcut to the Drupal administration screens.

Administration section:

After clicking on the wrench, the Drupal admin menu will appear on the left. The Drupal admin menu will look like the following screenshot:

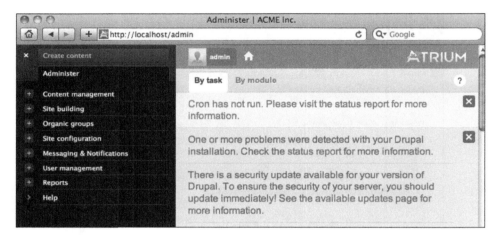

Clicking on the **x** next to **Create content** will close the administration sidebar. Clicking on a **+** next to any of the menu items will expand that menu to reveal additional tasks. On the right side we may see a set of messages that require our attention. The "green" messages are usually informational messages while the "red" messages indicate a part of our site that needs our attention.

When we first access the site, we will see the message **Cron has not run. Please visit the status report for more information**. Cron is a server task that should be run periodically and automatically by your server. This allows Drupal to perform routine housekeeping tasks including search indexing and checking for new updates.

 For more information on cron, visit `http://drupal.org/cron` which includes a tutorial for setting up cron including a short video.

We can click on the **status report** or locate the status report by clicking on **Reports** on the left and then clicking on **status report**.

The status report screen summarizes basic information about your Drupal site and identifies any potential issues that need to be addressed. In the following screenshot, we will see that under **Cron maintenance tasks** it says that it has never been run and provides a link to run cron manually:

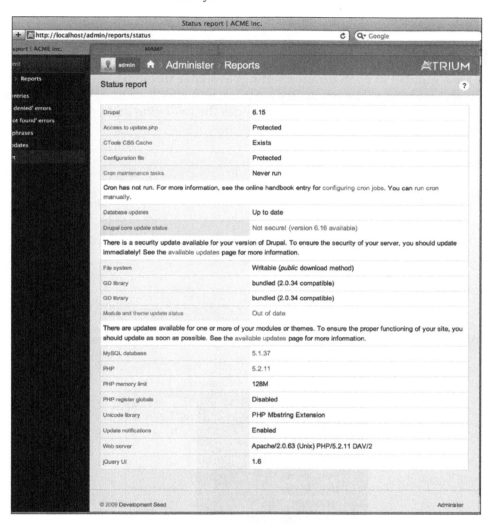

Click on the link **run cron manually**. The page will refresh and the time that cron was last run will be updated next to **Cron maintenance tasks**.

> You can always run cron manually by going to `http://siteurl/cron.php`. If you are using a local host, the URL would be `http://localhost/cron.php`. The `cron.php` has no output, so a blank page will appear once it is run. Then you can go back to your site using the site URL.

Administration menu

There are a number of configuration settings available through the Drupal administration menus. However, Open Atrium will handle most of the settings for us. The Drupal administration section includes the following sections:

- Create content
- Content management
- Site building
- Organic groups
- Site configuration
- Messaging & notifications
- User management
- Reports
- Help

The following screenshot shows the left-hand side of the administration menu:

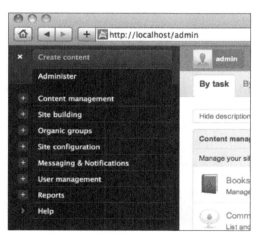

Create content

The **Create content** section is available in the Drupal administration section. However, Open Atrium prevents us from creating content through the backend as the distribution is designed for content to be entered through the Open Atrium installation. For other Drupal sites, without Open Atrium installed, you would create the majority of your content for your site using this link.

Content management

The **Content management** section provides additional options for configuring content. The most important one here is the **Content** section. This allows us to find a specific piece of content and edit it directly through the backend. This may be necessary sometimes when we need to tweak or unpublish a piece of content.

Site building

In the **Site building** section, you will have options to modify or create the following items:

- Blocks
- Context
- Features
- Menus
- Modules
- Themes

Again, a majority of the administration will be done through Open Atrium. If you are interested in what is going on behind the scenes, you can review the options in this section. Clicking on the Modules link for instance, will show you a list of all the modules used to build Open Atrium.

Organic groups

This section provides the core foundation for Open Atrium to provide subsets for each of our departments in our Acme Inc. corporation example. The Human Resources department is configured as an organic group on the backend. Fortunately, Open Atrium simplifies the creation and access of groups, and we will probably never need to do any configuration in this section.

Site configuration

The **Site configuration** section contains a number of configuration settings. The key elements in this section are the **Site information** and the **Performance** sections. Under the **Site information** section, we can configure the site name and e-mail address should they need to be changed. The performance section contains settings for caching and bandwidth optimization. For now, we will keep the default settings.

Messaging & notifications

This section provides a backend interface to handle subscriptions, messaging templates, and notification settings.

User management

The **User management** section provides an interface to manage Permissions, Roles, and Users. We may occasionally need to come to this section to reset a password or disable a user account.

Reports

The **Reports** section is our gateway to review recent log entries and errors that may be occurring on our site. This is also where we can run the status report and check for available updates. All of the updates for Open Atrium will be provided through the Open Atrium installation, and we will never need to update a module individually. However, this information can be helpful when troubleshooting a particular problem with a module.

Help

Throughout the administration sections, Open Atrium inline help messages are displayed wherever possible providing us with additional information about a specific topic. The help section expands on the inline help and provides us with a list of topics that we can read to better understand how a particular feature works.

Summary

Congratulations, we now have a working installation of Open Atrium. In Part I, we created a new database for our Open Atrium installation. Part II then covered downloading the Open Atrium distribution, and running the browser-based installation of Open Atrium. The last section, Part III, gave a brief overview of the Drupal administration sections and highlighted specific tasks including the following:

- Running cron
- Status report
- Site configuration
- User management

In the next chapter, we will focus on user administration and will walk through the process of creating and managing users. We will also discuss user roles and how they integrate with Open Atrium.

4
User Administration

At this point, we should now have a working installation of Open Atrium. The hardest part is setting up the web server and installing Open Atrium. Now, we are about to embark on the fun part, creating new users, and customizing Open Atrium for our use. In this chapter, we will walk through creating users and roles for your website. You may want to create your departments and groups first. By doing this, you can then add your users to their specific groups as you add them. To create the groups or departments first you can skip ahead to *Chapter 6, Groups* and return to this chapter when you are done creating groups. In this chapter, we will cover the following topics:

- User management
- User administration tasks
- User roles

User management

Open the browser and navigate to our newly created website. For Mac (MAMP) and Windows (WAMP) users the URL should be `http://localhost/`. You will probably already be logged in as the administration account from when we set up the site. If not, you will probably already be on the login page where you can go ahead and log in. If you do not see the login page, then click on the login link at the upper left corner of your site. Once you are logged in, you should see the main dashboard screen, which should look like the following screenshot:

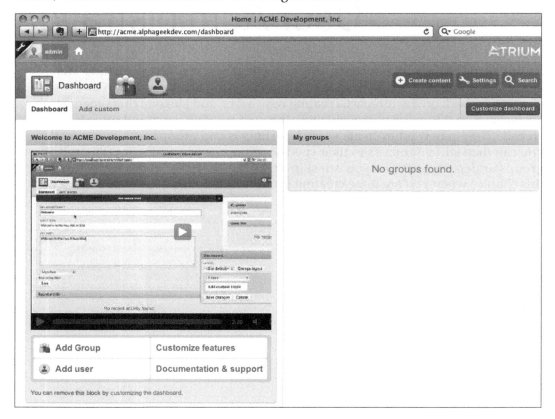

Adding a user

The first thing we will do is add a couple of users to our website. We can access the **Add user** screen in one of three ways. From the dashboard, we can click on the **Add user** link at the bottom left of the page. Alternatively we can click the member icon on the dashboard main menu. The areas highlighted in the following screenshot represent the two links. If you click on that icon, you will see an additional link of **Add user**, which you can click on the secondary menu.

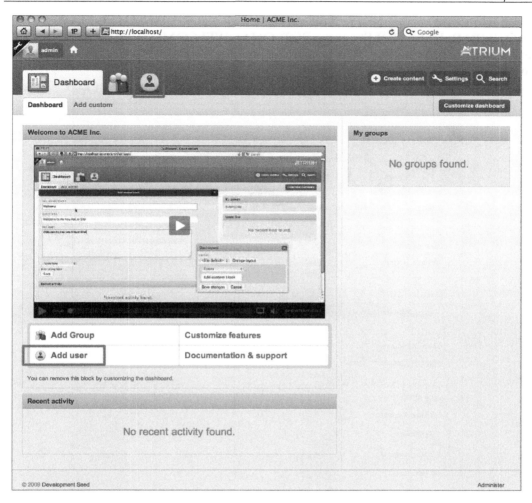

To add users, we will need to know the username and the e-mail address of the user that you are creating. For the username, I would recommend using the user's first name with a space and then the last name. This will allow your users to recognize other users quickly when reviewing comments, blog posts, and other postings.

On the following screen, we will fill out the **USER NAME, E-MAIL, E-MAIL (CONFIRM), USER ROLES,** and a **PERSONAL WELCOME MESSAGE.** In this example, I've pre-filled the information for one of my employees William Knight and assigned him to the manager role.

After we define additional roles and groups, we will see more options under the **USER ROLES** and **Groups** sections. Once all the information is filled out, we can go ahead and click on **Add**. We should then see a message similar to the following explaining that the user account has been set up and an e-mail has been sent with further instructions:

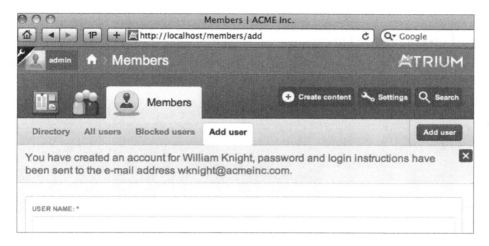

A "Personal Welcome Message" is appended to the beginning of the e-mail that is sent to the user when their account is created. The user will receive the instruction e-mail with a username and temporary password, which will suggest the user change their password after their first time logging in.

Go ahead and repeat this process and create two additional users. To follow along, you can use the same users that we are using in the book or create your own users. For the examples in this book, we will create two additional users, using their first and last names as their usernames. If you have logged out, make sure that you are logged in as an administrator to continue adding users.

User two

- **User Name:** Stephen Lawrence
- **E-Mail:** slawrence@acmeinc.com
- **User Roles:** Admin

User three

- **User Name:** Robert Lewis
- **E-Mail:** rlewis@acmeinc.com
- **User Roles:** None (other than default)

Member directory

Now, we can click on the **Members** navigation on the main navigation bar, and we should see a list of users similar to the following screenshot:

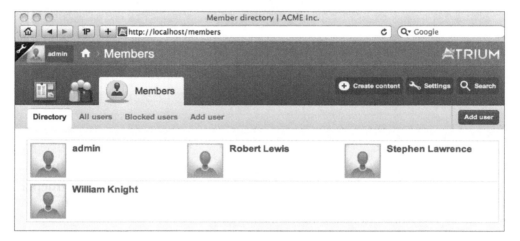

The preceding screen is known as the *Directory* screen and will list the usernames and pictures of each user on your website.

All users

Clicking on the **All users** navigation will provide you with an alphabetical list (by username) of each user along with their Groups and Roles. We can then click on individual users to go to their profile page and begin to make additional edits. The following screenshot shows an example of the *All users* list:

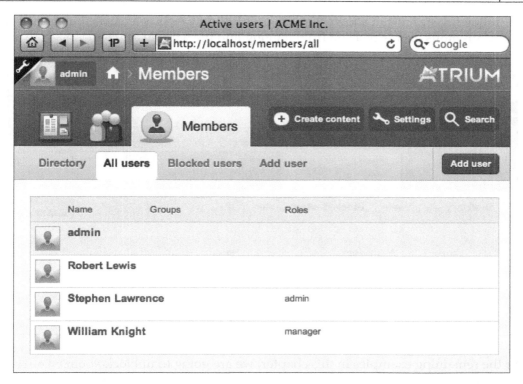

Blocked users

Blocked users will show you a list of any users whose status has changed from
`Active` to `Blocked`. One example of when you might want to block a user is when
someone leaves your company. They may have contributed content authored by
them. To maintain a historical reference and not lose this, you can block the user
instead of deleting them. This will prevent the user from logging in, but keep their
user account and any content that they have contributed. You can mark a user as
blocked by going into their **Account settings** and selecting **blocked** for their status,
or you can click on the **suspend** tab and then click on the **Confirm** button to suspend
or block the user when viewing the User profile page.

The following screenshot shows that our user **Robert Lewis** is a blocked user. Also, the **Anonymous** user is blocked from logging into the website as well:

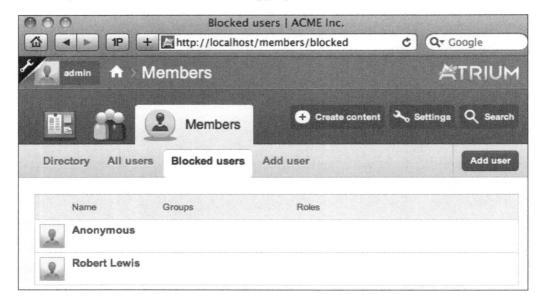

For the remaining examples in this chapter, we are going to unblock Robert Lewis. From the blocked users screen click on **Robert Lewis**, then click on **Account settings**. Under the **User administration** section, you will see a **Status** section where we will select the **Active** radio box, and then just above the **User administration** section, click on **Save** to save your changes. The following screenshot provides an example of where to change the user's status from "Blocked" to "Active":

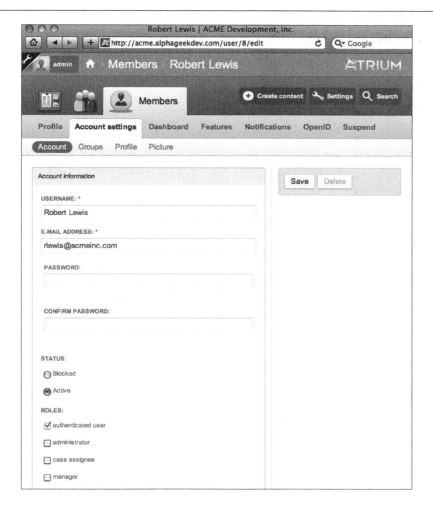

The next section will go into more detail about the various secondary tasks available to you when you are viewing a member's profile page.

User admin tasks

In this section, we will walk through examples and screenshots of each of the secondary tasks available for each user. They include the following:

- Profile
- Account settings
- Dashboard
- Features
- Notifications
- Overrides
- Suspend

Profile

From any of the directory screens where there is a user list, we can click on an individual user and begin to edit their settings. The following screenshot is an image of the secondary tasks for Robert Lewis just after clicking on his name in one of the directory screens:

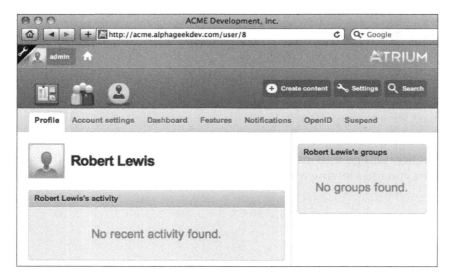

As we begin to add more information about the user, that information will be displayed on the preceding profile screen.

Account settings

Clicking on **Account settings** takes us back to the same page where we unblocked `Robert Lewis`. The following is a set of tertiary tasks that are exposed, including:

- Account
- Groups
- Profile
- Picture

Each of these screens provides additional fields to collect information about the user. The **Account** tab is where you can change the user's password, username, or e-mail address and select any additional roles that user should belong to. If you skipped ahead and already defined groups, then any groups the user belonged to will be listed under the **Groups** tab. The two most important items for now will be the **Profile** and **Picture** tabs.

Profile

There are actually two **Profile** tabs, which might seem a little confusing at first. The first one we went over is just a summary of the user account that we are reviewing. The second one is the one that actually allows you to enter additional profile information about the user. The first Profile is on the secondary menu bar, while the second instance is on the tertiary menu bar just below the second one.

The following is a screenshot of the secondary and tertiary task bars for the user Robert Lewis while viewing the **Profile** tab. We've already filled out the necessary information:

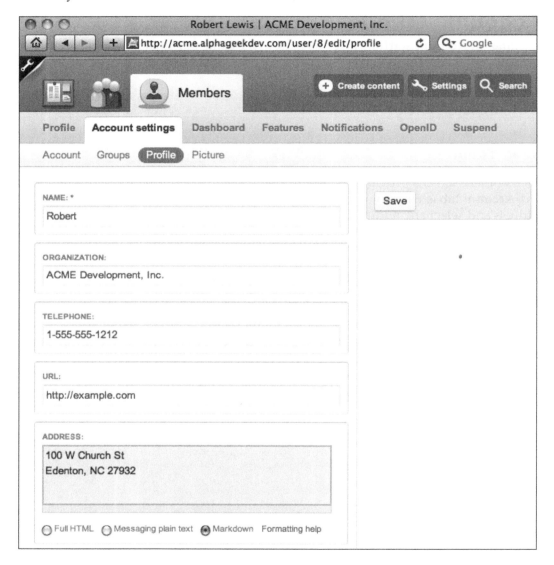

Go ahead and enter the information for your example user and then click on **Save** at the top right-hand column or at the bottom. The profile will be saved and we should see a message that the **Profile for Example User has been saved**. If we then click on the **Profile** option on the secondary menu to the left of **Account Settings**, we should see that Robert's information has been populated as indicated in the following screenshot:

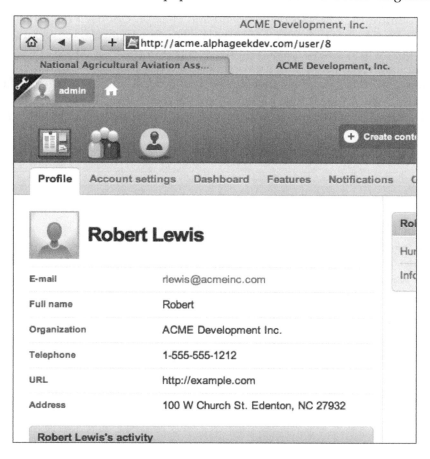

Picture

Now we can click back on the **Account settings** tab and then click on **Picture**. The **Picture** tab allows us to upload a picture for a user. If we hover over the **Upload Picture** section, we will see a message that defines the requirements for the picture. The message says **Your virtual face or picture. Maximum dimensions are 500x500 and the maximum size is 500kB**. Go ahead and click on **Choose File**, which will allow us to select a picture from our computer. For this example, we can use any picture to represent the user. After locating the appropriate file then click on the **Save** button to upload the picture. Do not worry about your picture being too big as long as it is under the 500x500 requirement. A Drupal module called "Image Cache" will automatically reduce the picture to the appropriate size depending on where it is displayed on the site. The following screenshot shows an example of the *Picture* page after we have uploaded a picture:

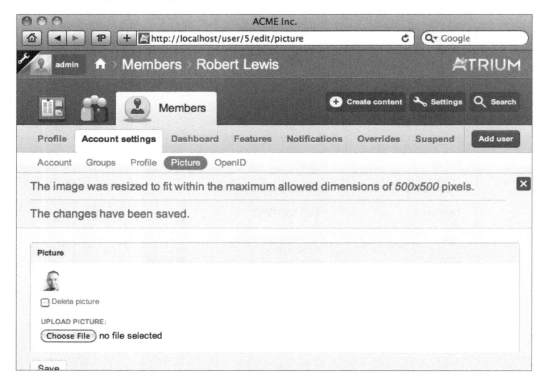

We should see a message provided by the "Image Cache" module that states that the picture has been resized. We should also see a message that the changes have been saved. Now, when we go to any of the directory pages, you will see the person's picture instead of a generic icon as shown in the following screenshot:

If you do not see a picture right away, you may need to insure that your files directory has read & write permissions (777) for Open Atrium to create and save the resized image. You can go to the report status to verify whether your file permissions are set correctly (**Administer** | **Reports** | **Report**).

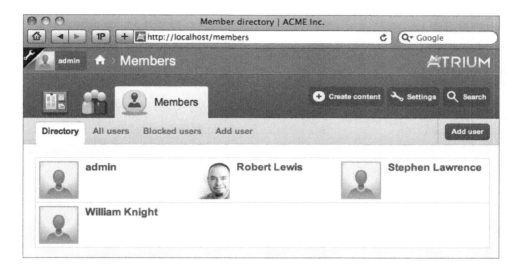

OpenID

The **OpenID** tab allows you to associate users with one or more OpenIDs for the user. An OpenID is a decentralized standard for authenticating users across multiple sites. It allows users to log in across multiple sites without entering a password and to use the same digital ID among the various sites.

 For more information visit the following URL:
`http://en.wikipedia.org/wiki/Open_id`

Dashboard

The Dashboard section allows you to configure and create additional dashboards for each user. Click on a member from one of the member directories and then click on **Dashboard**, which is in between the **Account settings** tab and **Features** tab on the first menu bar if you are logged in as an administrator. In the following screenshot, a custom dashboard has been created called Cases:

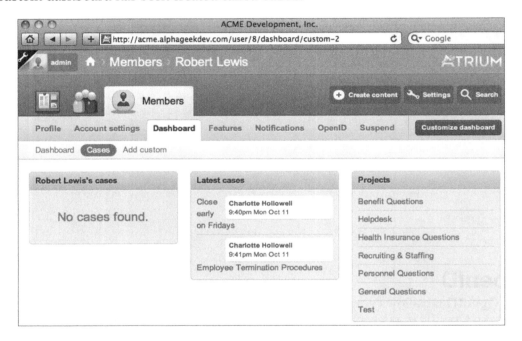

We created this dashboard by clicking on **Add custom** and providing a name for the new dashboard. Then we clicked on the **New dashboard** and clicked on the **Customize** dashboard on the top right. This allows us to choose the content we want on the dashboard and drag it to specific areas allowing us to arrange content in any form that we want. Now, when Robert Lewis logs in, he will have a custom dashboard called Cases available on his menu bar. This provides extreme flexibility for your users to arrange information the best way they see fit.

Features

The features section is a space on the members account page to add configuration sections for specific features. In our installation, the only additional feature that we have installed is "Spaces", which is provided in the core of Open Atrium. Spaces enable each of the members to have multiple dashboard pages. The following screenshot shows an example of the *Features* section on the account pages:

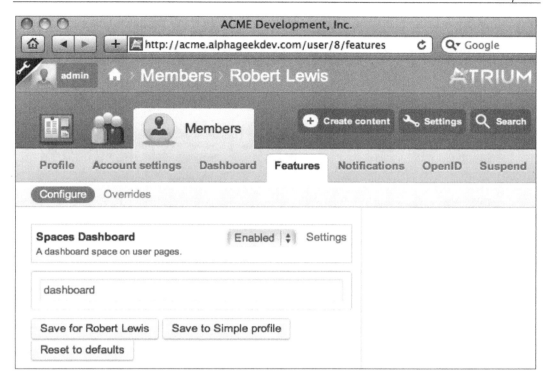

Notifications

The notifications section displays the current status for any notifications you are subscribed to and how those subscriptions are delivered. This section actually contains two subtasks that are available. The **Overview** section allows users or administrators to administer subscriptions, cancel subscriptions, and edit notification settings. The **Subscriptions** tab allows members or administrators to view all the subscriptions that a user has subscribed to.

 You can find more information about notifications on the Open Atrium community site at the following URL:

https://community.openatrium.com/documentation-en/node/28

The following screenshot shows an example of the *Overview* page for subscriptions:

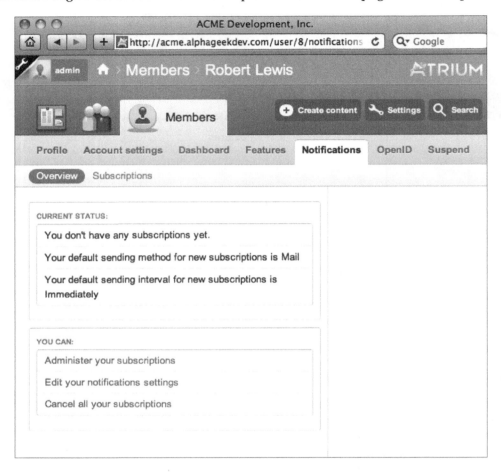

Suspend

As mentioned earlier in this chapter, we have an option to suspend a user from logging in to the server. This would be useful if we had to let someone go, and didn't want to delete all their content, but did want to prevent them from logging in. All we have to do is locate and click on the user in the member directory and then click on the **Suspend** tab and click **Confirm**, as shown in the following screenshot:

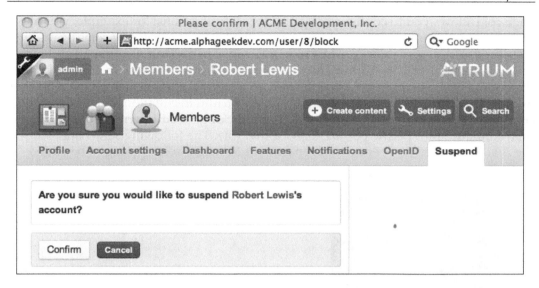

User roles

Open Atrium out of the box comes with four predefined roles, which are as follows:

- Anonymous user
- Authenticated user
- Admin
- Manager

If your organization structure warrants it you may wish to add additional roles. However, adding additional roles may make it more difficult to update your installation of Open Atrium with a future release. The role instructions are exactly the same for a normal Drupal installation without Open Atrium and examples are provided here strictly for reference.

Each role allows you to configure a special set of permissions; for example, you may want to add a simple *employee* role or expand the levels of *managerial* roles by adding a *Department Manager* role. To add a new role, you can click on the wrench at the upper left. Then click on **Administer | User management | Roles**. In the text box at the bottom of the list, you can type the new role name and then click on the **Add role** button. This will add the new role in our Open Atrium installation and allow us to configure special permissions for that role. By clicking on **edit permissions**, we can then configure the specific permissions for that role. The following screenshot shows the *Add Role* screen just before the **Department Manager** role is going to be added:

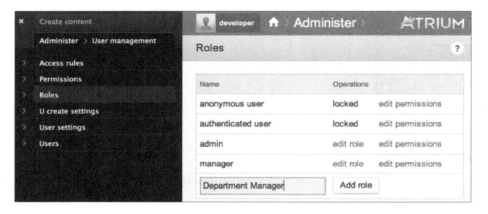

Summary

This chapter covered the basics of user administration, including how to add users and view the member directory to list active and blocked users. We then covered the various user administration tasks, including how to edit/add a profile, and configure account and notification settings. The last section of the chapter walked through an example of adding a new role to your Open Atrium website.

In the next chapter, we will cover the different types of dashboards and how they are modified, managed, and handled in Open Atrium. Groups will allow us to create subsites for each of our departments or sections depending on our organizational structure.

5
Dashboard

The dashboard is a central place to view a snapshot of the activity happening within your departments. This chapter will explain the three different types of dashboards and how to add custom content to a dashboard.

The chapter is divided into the following five sections:

- Main dashboard
- Group dashboard
- User dashboard
- Modifying Layout
- Boxes

Main dashboard

The main dashboard provides an interface for managing and monitoring our Open Atrium installation. This dashboard provides a central place to monitor what's going on across our departments. It will also be used as the central gateway for most of our administrative tasks. From this screen we can add groups, invite users, and customize group dashboards. Each individual who logs in also has the main dashboard and can quickly glance at the overall activity for their company. The dashboard is laid out initially by default in a two column layout. The left side of the screen contains the **Main Content** section and the right side of the screen contains a **Sidebar**. In a default installation of Open Atrium, there will be a welcome video in the **Main Content** area on the left. The first thing that you will notice when you log in is that there is a quick video that you can play on your main dashboard screen. This video provides a quick overview of Open Atrium for our users, and a review of the options you have for working with the dashboard. In the following screenshot, you will see the main dashboard and how the two separate content areas are divided, with a specific section marked that we will discuss later in the chapter:

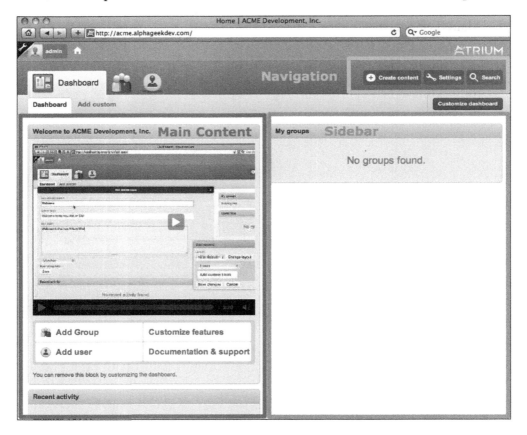

Each dashboard can be customized to either a two-column or split layout, as shown in the preceding screenshot, or a three-column layout. Under the *Modifying Layout* section of this chapter, we will cover how to change the overall layout. As you can see in the preceding image, the dashboard is divided into three distinct sections. There is the header area which includes the Navigation tabs for creating content, modifying settings, and searching the site. Under the header area, we have the main content and sidebar areas. These areas are made up of blocks of content from the site.

These blocks can bring forward and include different items depending on how we customize our site. For example, in the left column we could choose to display **Recent Activity** and **Blog Posts**, while the right column could show **Upcoming Events** and a **Calendar**. Any of the features that we find throughout Open Atrium can be brought forward to a dashboard page. The beauty of this setup is that each group can customize their own. In the next section of this chapter, we will cover group dashboards in more detail. However, the same basic concepts will apply to all the dashboards. After our users are comfortable with using Open Atrium, we may decide that we no longer need to show the tutorial video on the main dashboard. This video can be easily removed by clicking on the **Customizing the dashboard** link just above the **Recent Activity** block or by clicking on the **Customize dashboard** link on the top right in the header section. Click on the **customizing the dashboard** link and we will see a dashboard widget on the screen. This will be the main interface for configuring layout and content on our dashboard. Now, hover over the video and on the top right you will see two icons. The first icon that looks like a plus sign (**+**) indicates that the content can be dragged. We can click on this icon when hovering over a section of content and move that content to another column or below another section of content on our dashboard. The **X** indicates that we can remove that item from our dashboard. Hovering over any piece of content when you are customizing the dashboard should reveal these two icons.

The two icons are highlighted in the following screenshot with a square box drawn around them:

To remove the welcome video, we click on the red **X** and then click on **Save changes** and the video tutorial will be removed from the dashboard.

Group dashboard

The group dashboard works the same as the main dashboard. The only difference is that the group dashboard exposes content for the individual departments or groups that are setup on our site. For example, a site could have a separate group for the Human Resources, Accounting, and Management departments. Each of these groups can create a group dashboard that can be customized by any of the administrators for a particular group. The following screenshot shows how the Human Resources department has customized their group dashboard:

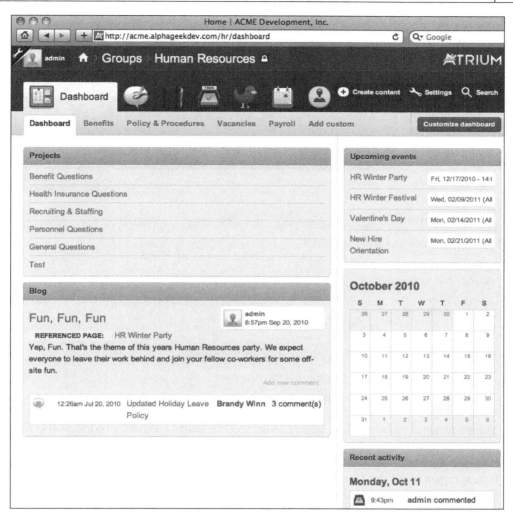

In the preceding screenshot, we can see how the HR department customized their dashboard. In the left column they have added a **Projects** and a **Blog** section. The **Projects** section links to specific projects within the site, and the **Blog** section links to the detailed blog entries. There is also a customized block in the right column where the HR department has added the **Upcoming events**, a **Mini calendar**, and a **Recent activity** block.

The **Projects** section is a block that is provided by the system and exposes content from the **Case tracker** or **Todo** sections of the HR website. The **Upcoming events** section is a customized block that highlights future events entered through the calendar feature.

To demonstrate how each department can have a different dashboard, the following screenshot shows the dashboard for the Accounting department:

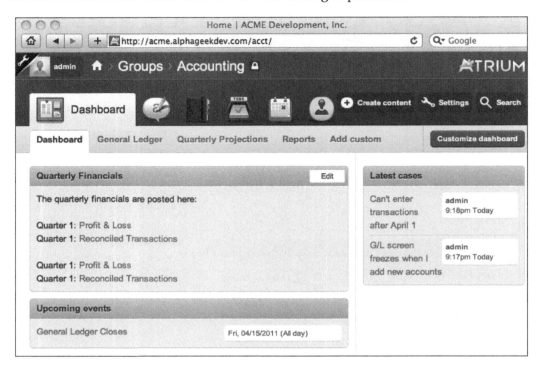

The Accounting dashboard has been configured to show a custom block as the first item in the left column, and below that a listing of **Upcoming events**. In the right column, the Accounting administrator has added a block which brings forward the **Latest cases** of all the latest cases, exposing the most recent issues entered into the tracking system. It is also worth noting that the Accounting department has a completely different color scheme from the Human Resources department. The color scheme can be changed by clicking on **Settings | Group Settings | Features**. We can scroll down to the bottom of the screen and click on **BACKGROUND** to either enter a hexadecimal color for our main color or pick a color from the color wheel as displayed in the following screenshot:

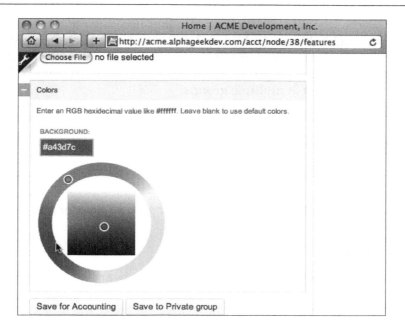

Spaces

Spaces is a Drupal API module that allows sitewide configurable options to be overridden by individual spaces. The spaces API is included with our Open Atrium installation and provides the foundation for creating group and user configurable dashboards. Users can then customize their space and set settings that are only applied to their space. This shows the extreme power and flexibility of Open Atrium by allowing users to apply customizations without affecting any of the other areas of Open Atrium. Users can use the functionality provided by spaces to create an individualized home page.

Group spaces

Group spaces provide an area for each group or department to arrange content in a contextual manner that makes sense for each group. In the preceding examples, the content that is important to the accounting department is not necessarily important to the human resources department. Administrators of each department can take advantage of Open Atrium's complete flexibility to arrange content in a way that works for them.

In *Chapter 6, Groups*, we will walk through the steps necessary to create individual groups as well as highlight some additional group features. Each Open Atrium installation can have an unlimited number of groups, thus providing the flexibility to grow your site as needed. Each group that is created will have its own unique URL and users can be members of multiple groups.

The URLs in the example that we have been looking at are listed as follows:

- Human Resources: `http://acme.alphageekdev.com/hr`
- Accounting: `http://acme.alphageekdev.com/acct`

Each URL is composed of the site URL, that is, `http://acme.alphageekdev.com/` and then the short name that we provided for our group space, hr and acct.

User spaces

User spaces work in the same way that the group dashboard and spaces work. Each user of the system can customize their dashboard any way that they see appropriate. The following screenshot shows an example of the user's dashboard for the admin account:

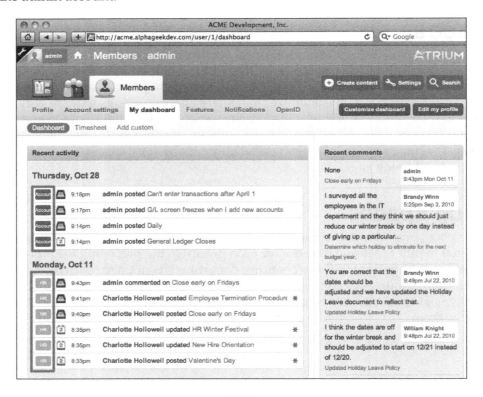

In the preceding screenshot, we have drawn a box around two areas. These two areas represent two different group spaces showing on the user's dashboard page. This shows how content can be brought forward to various dashboards to show only what is important to a particular user.

Modifying the dashboard

In this section, we will go through the steps necessary to modify either a group or user dashboard. For this exercise we will create a new group, enable features, and then customize the group's dashboard. Start by clicking on the large dashboard icon as indicated in the following screenshot:

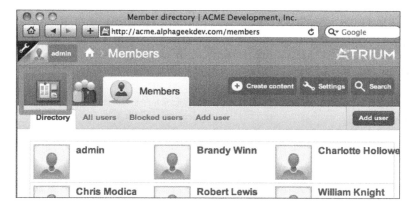

Now click on the **Create content** button on the far right and then click on **Group** as indicated in the following screenshot:

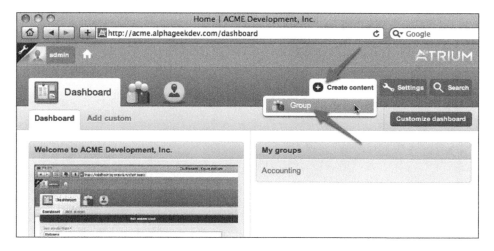

On the create group screen, we will provide a title and description for the group. Then we will assign the group a unique URL, so that it can be accessed directly. By default group spaces are considered private. On the group create screen, we will have the option to mark the group as public or private.

Private group

A private group is accessible only to users added to that group by one of the group's managers.

Public group

A public group is accessible to all users on the site. Users can join and leave public groups freely.

Examples of a private group would be the Human Resources and Accounting groups. These groups are only accessible by users who have been given explicit membership to the group. A public group would be open to anyone in the company to join. For example, we might want to create the following publicly accessible groups:

- Social activities
- Initiatives
- Company events

For now, we will create a private group for the Information Technology department. Fill out the group create form, as indicated in the following screenshot:

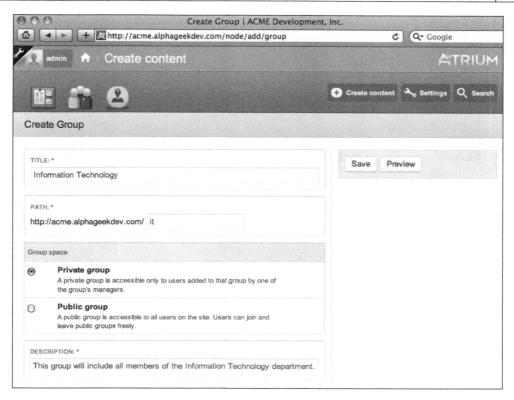

The fields should contain the following:

Title: `Information Technology`

Description: This group will include all members of the Information Technology department.

Path: `http://acme.alphageekdev.com/it` (your URL may be different)

Select **Private group**

Click on **Save**.

You can optionally add/change the author information. This option is useful if you have an administrator setting up a number of group sites and would like to designate a different user as a "group manager" for a particular site.

After clicking on **Save**, the browser should refresh and we should be on the dashboard for the Information Technology group as shown in the following screenshot:

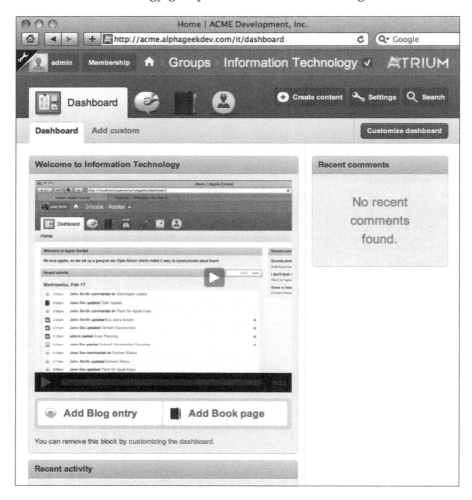

When you create new groups, the default dashboard layout is used to create the dashboard.

Layout

To change the layout of the dashboard, click on the **Customize dashboard** button that is just above the right column. You should then see a pop-up window that looks like the following:

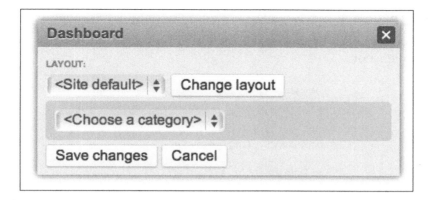

This pop-up may not be intuitive at first, but it is very powerful in allowing us to move items around. The first thing we want to do is expand the drop-down for Layout.

Here we have the following four choices:

- Site default
- Default
- Columns
- Split

Each of these options will select a different layout. For example, the Split option will split the page, so that there are two columns of equal width across the page. We will select a layout by clicking on **Change layout**. Similarly, we can try out each option. If we decide we do not like a particular layout, then we can click on **Customize dashboard** again after the page has been refreshed. You can try each option by clicking on **Customize dashboard** after the page has been refreshed.

Block items

The next customization that we will cover is what appears in each section on the group dashboard. Under the drop-down box we can review the list of components (features) that we can select from, to add a block related to that piece of content.

In this example, we will walk through setting up a mini calendar and adding a customize block containing a Message of the Day.

Calendar

In the drop-down under **Layout**, select **Atrium Calendar** as indicated in the following screenshot:

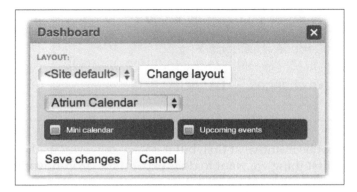

You will see two options just below the drop-down. Here you can drag and drop items directly onto the dashboard. In this case, we want to click on the **Mini calendar** item and drag it onto the column on the right side. We may have to try this a few times to get the positioning just right. Basically, all we have to do is drag the **Mini Calendar** over an area until we see the dotted box, as indicated in the following screenshot:

Once you have the dotted border, you can let go of the mouse button and the mini calendar will be inserted onto the page. Wait a second or two while the calendar is rendered and then click on **Save changes** on the layout pop-up. It may look a little weird and not like a calendar when it is first rendered, but once you click on **Save** it will show up like a regular calendar.

Message of the day

Click on **Customize dashboard** again, and then select **Boxes** in the category drop-down. We should see an option to **Add custom box**, as shown the following screenshot:

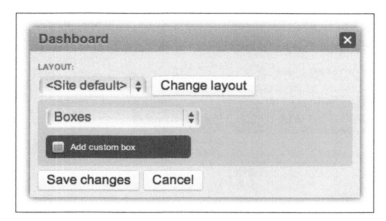

Now you can click on the **Add custom box** option and drag it over to the left column and drop it onto the page. After a couple of seconds, the box will change and allow you to add information for the block. Here you can add a **Box description**, **Title**, and **Body**. We also have the option of selecting an **Input format** which will allow us to insert text using **Full HTML**, **Markdown**, or **Plain text syntax**. To change the **Input format**, click on the plus sign (+) to the left of the **Input format** text to expand that section. We can click on the **Formatting help** link for additional information.

For this example, we can use the following values:

Box Description: Daily Message

Box Title: Message of the Day

Box Body: Type any message you like here

Click on **Save**.

Now, we can click on **Save changes** on the layout pop-up and our Message of the Day box will be added as indicated in the following screenshot:

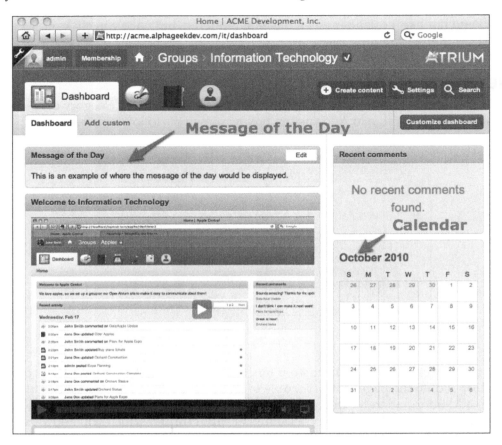

Now, we can continue to add additional blocks, and practice moving items around on the page. We can always click on **Cancel** on the **Dashboard layout** pop up.

Summary

In this chapter, we covered the basics of how to administer the **Dashboard** section of Open Atrium. Each site has a central dashboard, and each group or department within a site will have a built-in default dashboard. Then we learned about Spaces, which allow each group or user to override various site wide settings and create their own dashboard or space.

Then we went over how to create a group and how to modify the layout of the group's dashboard page. The layout is customized by selecting a particular layout from the drop-down menu and then clicking on **Save Changes**. Then we worked with the layout pop up to add a mini-calendar to the right sidebar, and add a custom block titled **Message of the Day** to the left column.

The next chapter, *Groups*, will go into more detail about how to use and administer groups on your site.

6
Groups

The ability to create groups is one of the core features of Open Atrium. When creating an intranet, it is important to be able to filter information for different audiences. Most companies that use Open Atrium will want to create a number of groups. A company may want to create at least one group for all of their employees and then individual groups for more specific workgroups, such as departments or projects. This chapter will walk through the different types of groups that can be created and provide guidance on how to manage groups.

In this chapter, we will cover the following topics:

- Importance of groups
- Organic groups
- Creating groups
- Archiving groups
- Administering group membership
- Joining a public group

Importance of groups

The ability to segregate information for a specific audience allows users to view information that directly relates to them. If all of the communications in an intranet project were in just one big group, users would become overwhelmed and eventually stop using the tool. Many organizations and companies are a composite of smaller departments or responsibility areas. This may correlate to departments, divisions, or workgroups in your company. Not only can Open Atrium be used to support a company's responsibility areas, it can also be used for specific projects that may be composed of members from several different areas of an organization. The ease and flexibility of adding groups to Open Atrium opens up a whole new way of organizing our intranet into logical entities. As we become more familiar with Open Atrium, we will begin to see additional opportunities to add groups or features that can potentially increase the efficiency in our organization. To demonstrate an example of how groups might be useful to an organization, we will take a look at the accounting department structured at ACME Inc. The following diagram is an organizational chart showing two levels of workgroups under the Accounting department:

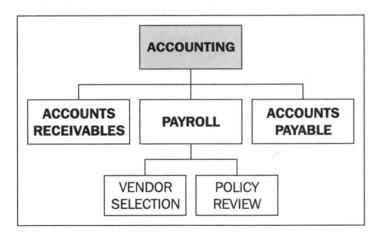

Each rectangle can be represented as a group in Open Atrium. A limitation of Open Atrium is that there is no concept of hierarchical groups where members of one group could automatically be included as members of another group. In our example, members of the **Payroll** group will have to be manually added to the **Accounting** group. In some ways this is more flexible because we might have employees who need to members of two or more workgroups.

Organic groups

One of the core features of Open Atrium is a Drupal module called **Organic groups**. The Organic groups (OG) module enables users to create and manage groups. The Organic groups module is used in many Social Media sites such as Pop Sugar (`http://www.popsugar.com`), Drupal (`http://groups.drupal.org`), and Fast Company (`http://www.fascompany.com/groups`). The key to the Organic groups module is that it hooks into node permissions to control who can create, edit, and delete content items. This mechanism allows Open Atrium to create restrictions on who can view/edit content for a particular group. If a group is set up as a private group and a particular user is not a member then they will not see any content created by that group. Organic groups also create a home page or dashboard for each group.

 To read more about Organic groups, you can visit the following website: `http://drupal.org/project/og`

Now that we have Open Atrium installed and understand how groups can be included in our intranet example, we will start by creating a few groups. To ensure that we build our intranet structure to reflect our company's workgroups, we should start by creating a rough sketch of how we want our groups to be organized. Let us start by creating a list of all the groups that we want all employees to have access to in our company. Then we can create a separate list for groups that will only be available to a limited number of employees. In the following example, the first column contains the name of the group we are creating while the second column contains the main department that the group belongs to. In the third column, we note the audience for the group, which will determine whether the group is created as a public or private group.

Group Name	Department	Audience
Accounting	Accounting	Accounting employees
Human Resources	Human Resources	HR employees
Payroll	Accounting	Only payroll employees
Accounts receivable	Accounting	Only A/R employees
Accounts payable	Accounting	Only A/P employees
Benefits	Human Resources	HR write access, all can read.

We will explore private and public groups in more detail in the following section named *Creating new groups*.

Creating new groups

To create a new group we first need to log in as an administrative user. We can use the user that we have created named admin. Once we are logged in, there are two places from where we can access the group creation screen. There will be a link about three quarters of the way down the page where we can click on **Add Group**, and there is also a **Create content** link drop-down menu towards the top right that will allow us to create a group. If you have already removed the Welcome video which included the **Add Group** link, you can use the **Create content** link to add your groups. The following screenshot highlights the two areas of the screen from where we can access the group creation links:

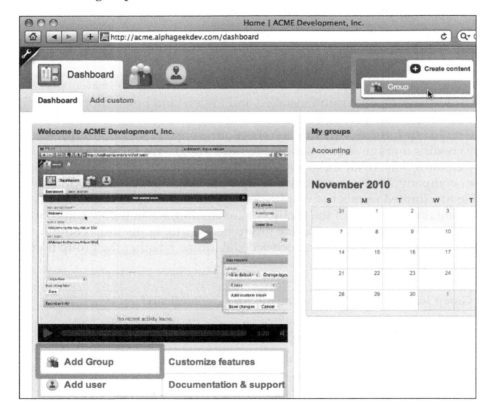

After clicking on the **Add Group** or **Create content | Group** links, we will be on the screen that allows us to get information about our group. Typically, in Drupal terminology this is refereed to as the "Node Edit" screen. This screen will vary slightly depending on what type of content we may be editing, but the basic structure of the screen will be maintained across Drupal sites. This screen is typically customized with additional fields or content areas to allow for different types of content to be entered. For example, a calendar event may use the "Node Edit" screen and will most likely have Title and Body fields in common with other content types. However, an event content item might also have fields for a start date and end date. In Drupal, this functionality is provided by a set of modules called **CCK (Content Construction Kit)**. In Drupal 7, the majority of the CCK functionality has been moved to the core installation of Drupal. If you are working on a Drupal 6 site, you will most likely want to download CCK and any supporting module. The Open Atrium distribution includes the CCK modules.

There are only a few fields that need to be filled out on this screen to create our first group. The **TITLE** field is the group name. Referring to the list we previously created, we will start with the Accounting group. After the **TITLE** field, there is a **PATH** field. This field allows us to set the default URL for our group's main dashboard page. For the Accounting group, we will choose **acct** as the path.

Under the **Group space** section, we can choose to make the group a **Private group** or **Public group**. For now, we will choose **Private group** to restrict access to only members of the Accounting department. After the **Group space** options, we have the **DESCRIPTION** field, which is a text field describing the group and its intended use. This can be any text to further clarify the group's purpose. The following screenshot shows the Accounting group page just prior to clicking on the **Save** button with all of the required fields filled out:

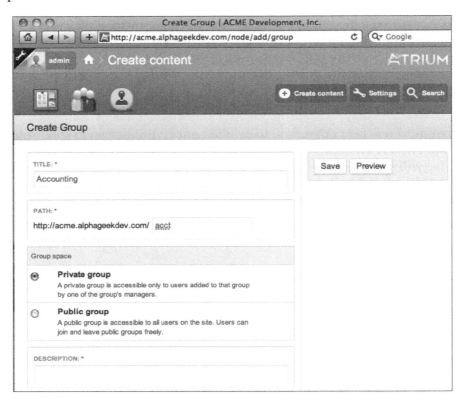

Once we've confirmed that we have entered all the information correctly, we can click on **Save** in the right column to create the Accounting group. The group will be created and we should now be directed to the group's dashboard page. We can see the URL for the page is `http://acme.alphageekdev.com/acct/dashboard` and can also be referenced as `http://acme.alphageekdev.com/acct`, as the dashboard is defaulted to be the home page for the group. Of course, for your site the the first part of the URL would be replaced with your sites address. The Accounting dashboard page should look like the following screenshot:

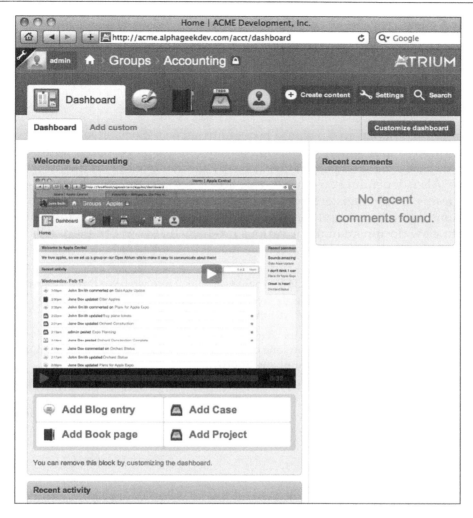

Private group

The definition of a private group is as follows:

A private group is accessible only to users added to that group by an administrator.

This type of group is useful for groups where we want the membership to be controlled, and content created in this group is only shared among group members. An example of this group is the "Accounting" department or "Human Resources" group where there is a defined set of users that have access to the content within these groups.

Public group

A public group allows any user of our Open Atrium installation to join that group. The definition of a public group is as follows:

> *A public group is accessible to all users on the site. Users can join and leave public groups freely.*

An example of a public group would be a group such as "Social Events" or "Recreation Activities" where any user could choose to be a part of these groups. Users can choose to participate in these groups and remove or add themselves at any time. Also, depending on our sitewide access settings, we can choose to expose public groups to only registered users who have an account on our system, or to anonymous users. An example of this could be where we want anonymous users to be able to view documentation for various products that your company sells.

To modify sitewide access settings, go to: `http://www.example.com/features` and scroll down to Site settings. Here we have three options:

- Private access only — only members who have been manually added to Open Atrium can access the site.
- Public access, open registration — some pages and groups are set to public where anyone can view the content. Members can sign up for access without any approval.
- Public access, moderated registration — some pages and groups are set to public where anyone can view the content. Members can sign up for access but require an approval before they are granted access settings.

We can access the settings menu from the Accounting dashboard by clicking on **Settings** in the upper right navigation. The settings menu contains the following options:

- Group settings
- Customize features
- Reorder menu
- Archive
- Members

The following is a screenshot of the settings menu:

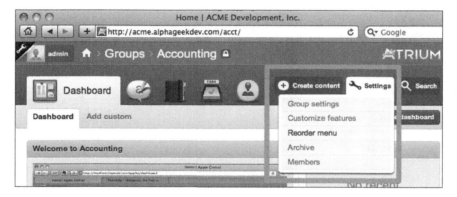

Group settings

To modify any of the group settings, we can click on **Settings** at the upper right and select **Group settings**. This screen will look exactly like the screen we used to add new groups. Here we can modify the title, path, description, and public or private settings.

Customize features

The next item under **Settings** is the **Customize features** section. The following screenshot shows an example of the Customize features screen:

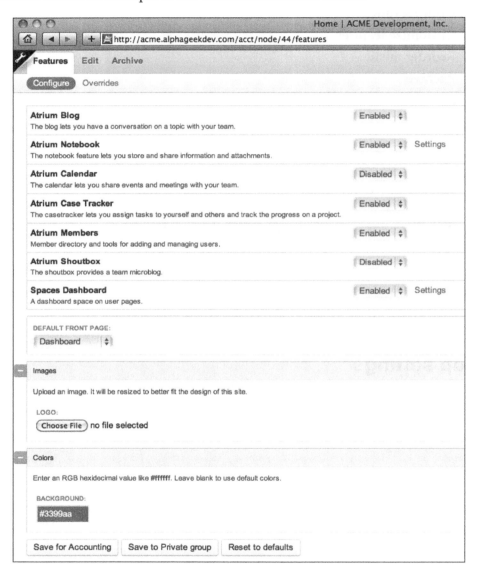

This will be one of the key configuration screens for our group. Here we can do the following:

- Enable and disable specific features
- Define the front page
- Upload images
- Modify background colors

Enabling and disabling specific features

This section allows you to define what features you want available to your group. As more features are developed and added to your Open Atrium installation, they will appear here. Out of the box the following features are available:

- Atrium Blog
- Atrium Notebook
- Atrium Calendar
- Atrium Case Tracker (To Do List)
- Atrium Members
- Atrium Shoutbox
- Spaces Dashboard

The following screenshot is an example of the enable and disable features section:

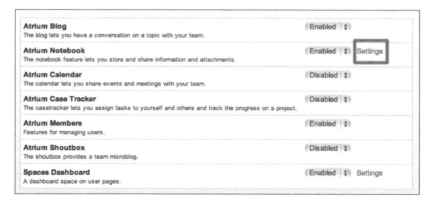

To toggle a features status just select the drop-down and choose the correct status. Also, some of the features will provide additional configuration which can be changed using the **Settings** link next to the specific feature. For the Accounting departments page we will enable all of the features by toggling **Calendar**, **Case Tracker**, and **Shoutbox** to **Enabled**.

Default front page

This section allows us to choose which page users will see when they go to your departments URL. The default is set to show the "Dashboard" page. However, for some departments it may make more sense to select the "Blog" or "Notebook" page. To change the default front page, just select a new item from the drop-down menu. The default front page section looks like the following:

Uploading images

The **Images** section allows us to upload an image or logo to be associated with this group. This will be displayed on the group's "Dashboard" page and other pages within the group section. It will help provide a visual cue that we are in a specific group or department's page. To upload an image, we can click on **Choose File** and a standard dialog box will appear allowing us to select an image from our computer. We do not need to worry about the exact logo size as the image will be resized automatically using a very powerful Drupal module called **Image Cache**.

 For more information about the Image Cache module, visit the following URL:
http://drupal.org/project/imagecache

The following screenshot shows how the Image section looks:

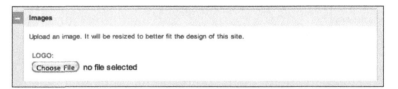

Modifying background colors

The **Colors** section allows us to specify a color scheme for our group or department. This will become important as we create more groups. It provides another visual cue to distinguish this group from the rest of the groups. By clicking on the color under the **Background** field, a color selector comes up where you can move the circles around to select a specific color. Some departments may already have their own color scheme in which you can use the RGB (Red, Green, Blue) hexadecimal number to define the color. The following screenshot shows an example of the color section:

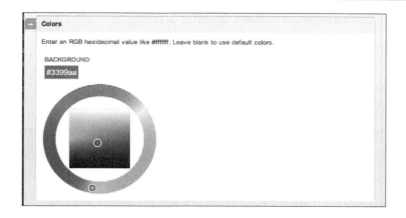

 Open Atrium uses Drupal's built-in color module. You can find out more information about the color module by going to the following URL:

`http://drupal.org/node/108459`

For more information about defining RGB colors visit the following URL:

`http://en.wikipedia.org/wiki/Web_colors`

Once we have made our changes we can click on **Save configuration** and the new customizations will be loaded for our group. If we make a mistake and want to revert back to the defaults, we can click on **Reset to defaults** and our changes will be reset to their original settings.

Reorder menu

The **Reorder menu** allows us to change the order of the icons on our group's page. This can improve usability for the department members by organizing the icons representing different features in the order of most used to least used. The following screenshot shows an example of the default icon order for the Accounting department page:

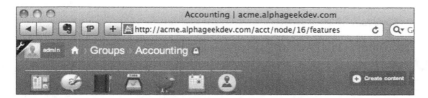

The icons by default are listed in the following order:

- Dashboard
- Blog
- Notebook
- Case Tracker (Todo list)
- Shoutbox
- Calendars
- Members

The following screenshot shows how the the **Reorder menu** options look:

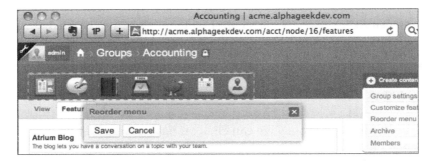

To reorder the icons, click on **Reorder menu** under the **Settings** section at the top right. We will then see a dotted border around the icon list and a dialog box to save or cancel changes.

It is not exactly obvious what to do here, but we will learn as we perform further customizations that anything with a dotted border around it is a cue that the items can be re-arranged or moved. To change the order of the icons, we can click and drag an icon to a new position on the icon toolbar and then click on **Save**. In the following screenshot, we can see that we moved the **Blog** and **Calendar** icons to the left of the dashboard icon:

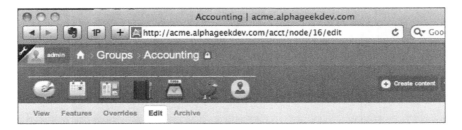

Archive

The **Archive** option simply allows us to archive a group that is no longer needed. The following screenshot shows an example of the **Archive** settings screen:

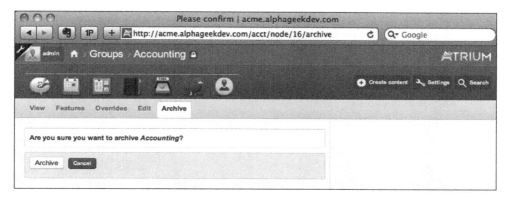

This would be useful where one of our groups might be a project that has finished. We do not want to delete the group because we may lose valuable information. By archiving the group, we can prevent adding of new content and still allow information about the project to be maintained. This would also be useful if our company merged two departments together. In that case, we could create a new group for the newly merged department and archive the two previous departments for reference.

To archive a group, click on the **Settings** link and then click on **Archive** from a group's dashboard page. A message will be displayed (as shown in the following screenshot) stating that the group is archived:

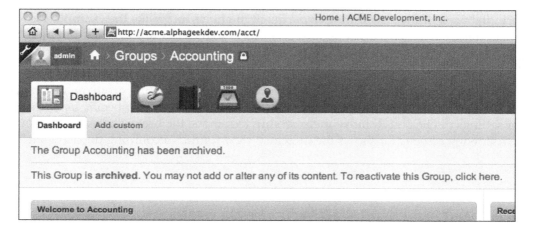

Members

The **Members** section allows us to manage our group members. The following screenshot shows the members screen for our Accounting department:

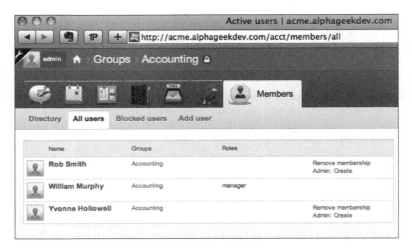

From this screen, we can do the following actions:

- Viewing the directory
- Viewing all users
- Viewing blocked users
- Adding users
- Adding users to group

The initial view of the Accounting department members looks like the example shown next. In this example, we've added three members to the Accounting department.

Viewing the directory

The **Directory** view simply lists all the members of the Accounting group and displays the user's picture if one was uploaded for them. You can click on a specific user to edit user settings or click on **Remove membership** to remove the user's access to the group. The following screenshot shows the directory view for the Accounting department:

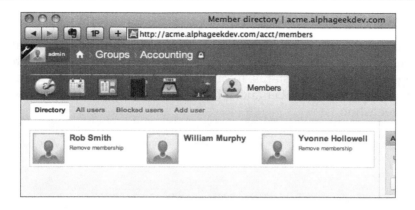

Viewing all users

This view also lists members of the current group, in this case, Accounting. The only difference is that this view is arranged in a list format with each group member on a separate row. The user picture is just to the left of each user and this table also shows the roles that the group members belong to. The following screenshot shows an example of the **All users** view:

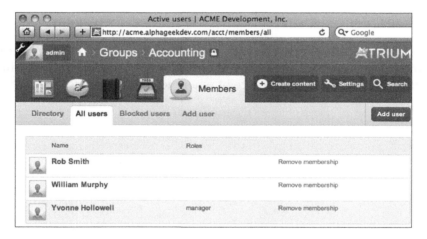

Viewing Blocked users

The **Blocked users** section lists any members of the Accounting group that have been suspended. This may be useful if we need to reactivate a member who has had a change in employment status. In our example, we show that Emma Gibson is currently a suspended member and is in the Accounting group, as shown in the following screenshot:

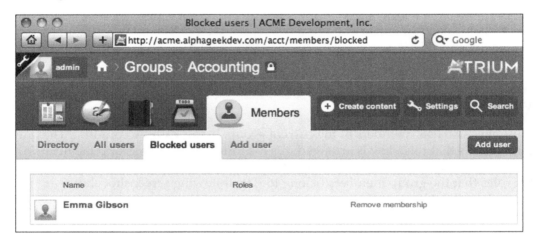

To reactivate Emma Gibson, we can click on her name and then click on **Account settings** and select **Active** for the status radio box under **Account information**. See the following screenshot for a reference of where to change the member's status:

Adding a user

We can also add new users to our intranet while we are in a group by clicking on the **Add user** link. This screen is exactly the same as the previous **Add user** screen discussed earlier in *Chapter 4, User Administration*. When adding a user through the **Members** screen of a group page, there is a bug where the user does not get added to the group you are viewing. To correct this, you will need to locate the user through the **Members** tab from the main dashboard and manually add them to the group. Until this bug is fixed, it is easier to just add members through the main dashboard.

Add existing users

This section is the key to adding existing members to the current group. It is located at the right sidebar whenever you are in the group member settings section. To add an existing user to the group, begin typing the first few letters of the username in the box and then select the user you want to add and click **Add to group**. The following screenshot shows an example of adding an existing user to the Accounting group:

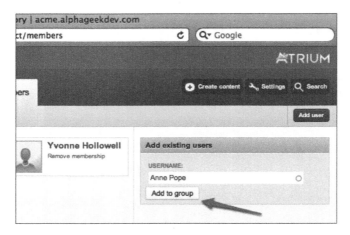

Joining a public group

It is not exactly obvious as to how an Open Atrium user who is not a manager of a group can join an open group. Ideally, you should be able to go the group's dashboard and click on the **Join Group** link. However, that option is not currently available in Open Atrium. To join a public group a normal user needs to log in. Then they need to click on their username on the top left and select **Account settings** under the drop-down menu. The following screenshot shows an example of this:

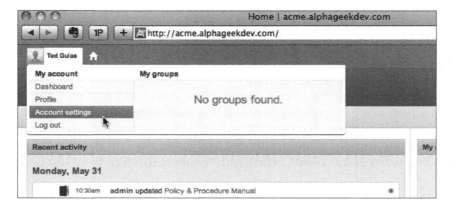

From the **Account settings** screen they need to click on the **Groups** item in the submenu. Here the public groups available in our Open Atrium system will be listed and the user can select the checkbox next to each group that they want to join and then click on **Save**. In our example, **Ted Gulas** has selected **Join Human Resources**, as shown in the following screenshot:

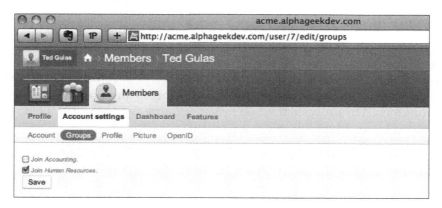

Now Ted can click on the **Groups** icon on his main menu and then click on **My groups** on the submenu and see that he is now a member of the **Human Resources group**. On this page, Ted can click on the **Human Resources** link to go directly to that group's dashboard page. The following image shows an example of Ted's **My groups** page:

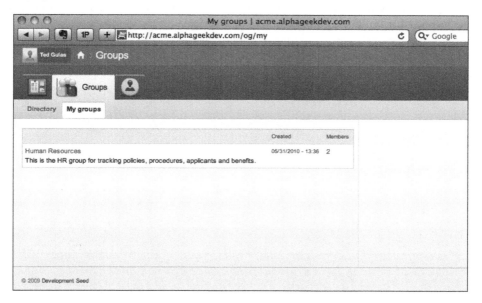

Summary

In this chapter, we covered the basics of how to manage, create, and configure Open Atrium groups. The first section of the chapter talked about the importance of groups and how they can be used to segregate information among a company's various departments. We discussed how Open Atrium supports groups by implementing the Organic groups module in Drupal.

The next section walked through the process of creating new groups and provided examples of how to configure the various settings available on the group's configuration page. This included a brief summary on how public and private groups work. Public groups are available to all members and possibly anonymous users of our Open Atrium system while private groups are only available to users who are added by an administrator to a particular group.

In the group settings section, we went over how to enable and disable specific features, how to modify the group's background color, and how to upload a logo for the group.

The next section covered group member management and how to view the group directory and add/remove members from a particular group. Finally, in the last section we covered how an Open Atrium user can add themselves to a publicly available group.

In the next chapter we look closely at how the document library, also referred to as *the notebook* or *wiki*, can be used to manage our documentation requirements and provide a space for collecting additional knowledge.

7
Document Library

The document library is referred to in Open Atrium as the **Notebook**. Its functionality is similar to the functionality of a Wiki. In Drupal, this functionality is provided by the "book" core module. This module allows us to structure content in a similar manner that we would structure a book. Notebooks can have volumes, chapters, pages, and subpages that maintain a hierarchy with one another, so that the content can be organized in a consistent manner.

In this chapter, we will cover the main features of the Notebook:

- Adding book pages and organizing them hierarchically
- Attaching files to pages, so that others can view them
- Tracking and reverting changes as necessary
- Archiving books that are no longer needed

Creating a new book

To demonstrate the features and functionality of Open Atrium's document library, also called Notebook, we will create an employee manual for the Human Resources department. In our example, we are going to go to the Human Resources dashboard located at ("/hr") and click on **Notebook**. On this page, there will be a button on the right side of the screen titled **Add Book page** which we can click on to start our employee manual. The Notebook screen looks like the following screenshot when you first click on it:

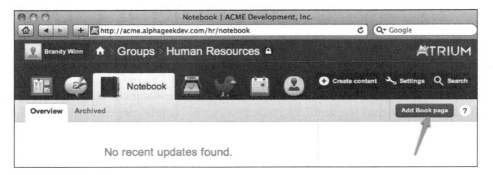

After clicking on the **Add Book page** button, we will see an edit screen similar to previous screen that we've looked at. The only difference on this screen is that there are a few new fields specific to creating a book page. On the edit screen, we see the normal fields:

- Title
- Body
- Notifications
- File attachments
- Keywords
- Revision information
- Save/Preview

In addition to the existing fields, we have an additional section for the **Book outline** which looks like the following screenshot:

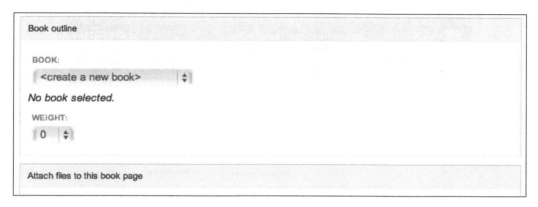

Here we should select **<create a new book>** because this is going to be our first top level page. If we were adding a page to an existing book, we would want to select the parent page for the new page we were adding from the drop-down menu. For this example, we will create a new book and use the following values for the fields:

- **Title**: Employee Manual
- **Body**: This manual is for all the employees at Acme, Inc. and will be updated as policies and effective dates change
- **Notifications**: Click on **Do not send notifications for this update**
- **Book outline**: Keep the defaults
- **Attach files to this book page**: None
- **Keywords**: Policy, Manual
- **Revision information**: Keep defaults

After we have filled out the form, it should look similar to the following screenshot:

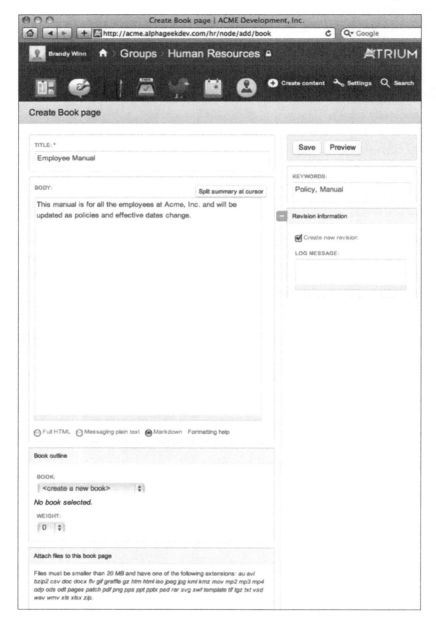

Once we have filled out the form, we can click on **Save** at the upper right-hand corner. If everything is saved correctly, the Employee Manual page will be displayed with options to do the following:

- Add child page
- Print
- Print entire section
- View
- Edit
- Archive
- Reference this
- Add Book page

At this point, we are on the main **Notebook** screen. If we were editing a page directly, we would also see a **Revisions** tab instead of the **Archive** tab. We can see from the following screenshot the various options and notice that our keywords are now listed under the **Tagged** label:

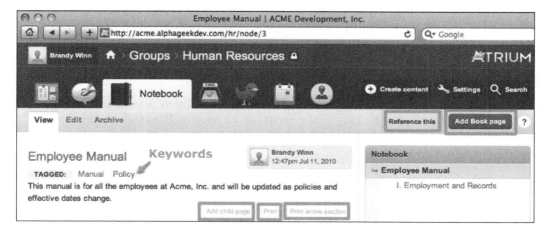

Adding a child page

Now that we have a book created for our employee manual, we can begin adding child pages to the book. A child page is a subpage from a parent page. The book module in Drupal allows this hierarchy to be maintained, so that a parent or top level page can have several child pages, and each child page can have their own child pages. In this example, the parent will be the book itself. Our employee manual will consist of several sections with additional child pages. This way the manual can be broken up into pieces and organized much like a printed version of an employee manual.

One of the nice things about Open Atrium is that the initial installation provides the basic features needed to utilize existing functionality. However, if you decide that you need additional information collected on your page, you can add additional fields for specific items. In *Chapter 11, Customization,* we will go into more detail about how to add additional fields to content.

For our employee manual example, we will create the following five sections:

- Employment and records
- Leave
- Employee benefits and awards
- Discipline/Appeals/Grievances
- Separation

To create our sections, we will add child pages with the employee manual as the main book or parent. Then within each section, we will create subpages (additional child pages) for the content needed. The first page of each section will contain an overview of the contents for that section.

Once we click on the **Add child page**, we will see a new form similar to the one we created for the book. The title of the create/edit page will be **Create Book page**. The only difference will be in the **Book outline** section. Here we will see the following options:

- Book
- Parent item
- Weight

The **Book** and **Parent item** sections allow us to determine where this page fits in with our overall book. The **Weight** item is used throughout the Open Atrium and Drupal system to determine the order that something appears.

 Note: A lower weight will float a particular item above items with higher weights. For example, a child page with a weight of one will appear before child pages with a weight of two or higher.

The following screenshot shows an example of our first child page filled out and ready to be saved:

The title of this form will be used to determine the main title of the section. In the **Book outline section**, we can see that for **book**, we have selected **Employee Manual** and for **Parent item**, we have selected **Employee Manual** with a **Weight** of zero. This will create a new child section in our book as the first section. Once we click on **Save**, we can then add more child pages for each section, or we can continue adding child pages for the current section. On the right-hand sidebar, a summary or table of contents for each of the pages will be displayed. The following screenshot shows an example of the **Table of Contents** along with the **Add child page** option:

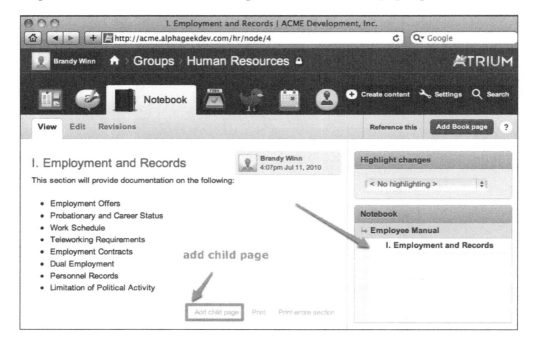

At this point, we should go ahead and create the additional pages for each section, so that we can start to see our employee manual come together. Click on **Add child page** and we will create pages for the remaining four sections:

- Leave
- Employee benefits and awards
- Discipline/Appeals/Grievances
- Separation

When we are creating our section pages, it will be important to select the **Employee Manual** in the **Parent Item** drop-down. This will maintain the manual's hierarchy for each section. One of the benefits of adding the sections is that we can add content in an order that makes sense for us and we arrange that content later. We can also parse out the responsibility of each section to other parties, and each person can maintain a particular section to insure that the employment manual stays updated.

The following screenshot shows an example of our **Table of Contents** after the five sections have been added:

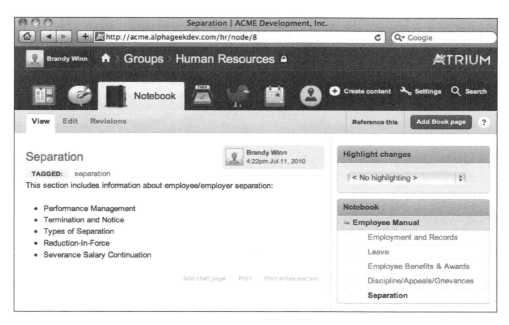

On the right-hand said, we begin to see the hierarchy of each section. After adding these sections, we may realize that it would be helpful to have section numbers for each section. To add section numbers, we can edit the title of each page to include the section number. However, we need to remember that if we add a new section in between sections, we will need to change the order of the sections by using the **weight** option.

To add the section numbers, click on a particular section in the table of contents and then click on **Edit**. Then we can add a Roman numeral in front of the title for each section.

This is a good example of when we would want to extend the functionality of the Book form. We could add an additional field towards the top of the document for Section number with a drop-down list of available section numbers. For more information see *Chapter 11, Customizations*.

The following screenshot shows how the table of contents looks after adding section numbers:

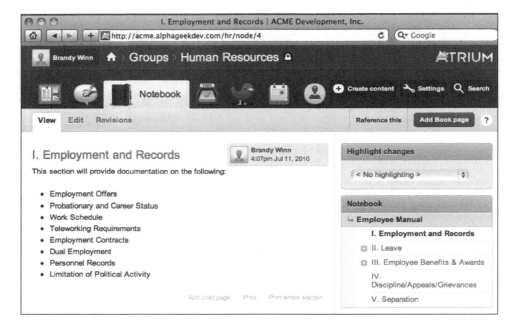

Revisions

Another important feature to note when moving from a paper based manual to an electronic based system is that we have the ability to track revisions. Open Atrium uses Drupal's standard revision tracking system with a few extra features. When you are reviewing a document and have edit privileges, you will see an option **Highlight Changes** just before the documents content, as shown in the following screenshot:

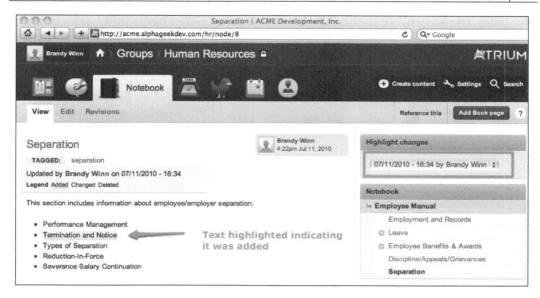

The square box on the top-right side indicates that we have selected a particular change to highlight. We can also see that **Termination and Notice** is highlighted indicating that this text was added with this revision. Also, we can click on the **Revisions** button to see a list of all revisions for the current document.

When we are editing a document, we will see a section for Revisions with an option defaulted to **Checked** for **Create new revision** and an option to add a note or **Log message** about the revision. In most cases, we will leave the **Create new revision** selected. However, in some cases we may not want to create a new revision. One example would be when we are fixing a typo in the document and not adding or revising any content.

The following screenshot highlights the Revisions section when editing a document:

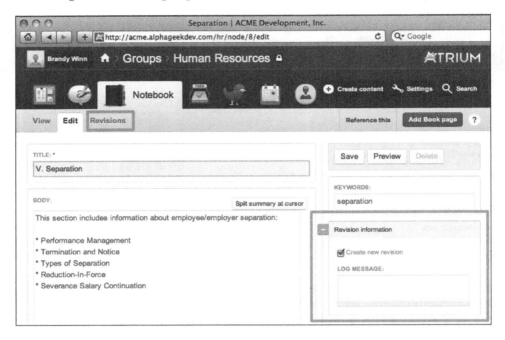

In this example, we've edited the Separation page to include an additional page named **Termination and Notice** as the second bullet point.

Highlight changes

While viewing a document, we can click on **Highlight changes** and the **Revisions** sidebar will appear showing the person that edited the document, the time and date it was modified, and if a **Log message** was entered. A legend will also appear showing the highlight color for items **Added**, **Changed**, or **Deleted**. By selecting a **Revision** in the drop-down menu under **Highlight changes**, the particular changes related to that revision will be highlighted in the appropriate color corresponding to the change.

In our example, we have selected the second revision by **Brandy Winn** dated **7/11/2010 – 16:34**, as shown in the following screenshot:

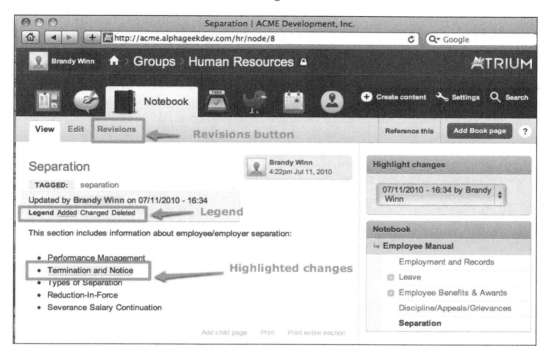

As we can see in the preceding screenshot, the **Termination and Notice** section is highlighted in green, indicating that this text was added in this revision. This is an important part of any document management system to be able to see and track changes for each document. This system enables us to identify what was changed, when it was changed, and who changed it.

Revisions tab

The second way to view revisions is to click on the **Revisions** tab on the menu bar just after the **View** and **Edit** tabs. This will show us a list of all the revisions for this document with radio boxes to select individual revisions. This also provides a mechanism to compare changes between revisions. In the first column of radio boxes, we select the original revision that we want to compare. In the second column, we select the revision that we want to compare with the first one. In the following screenshot, we have selected the first revision and the last revision to see all the changes that have been made since the document was created:

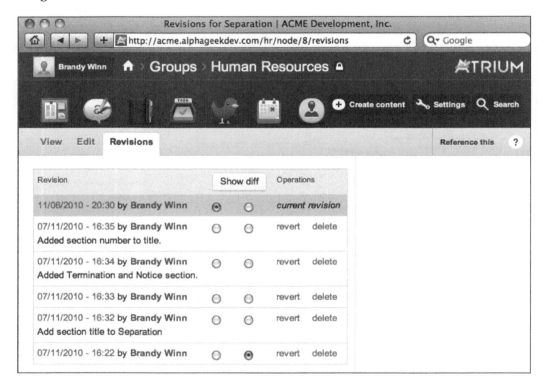

Now, by clicking on the **Show diff** button, we can see a list of all the changes from the first revision to the second revision. The first column will show what the text originally was while the second will show any new text that was added. The current revision will also be displayed just below it. As we can see, this is a very powerful feature to determine what has changed in each document. The following screenshot shows the revision screen after clicking on **Show diff**:

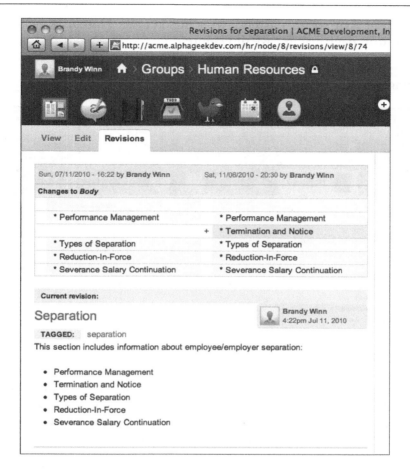

There is also a **Revert** option to revert the current revision to a particular revision. If we go back to the view page with the **Highlight changes** option, we will also see the highlighted changes after reverting. There is also a **Delete** option, but it permanently deletes a revision, so use it carefully.

Subpages

The next part to creating new documents and assembling our employee manual is to create a few subpages in our employee manual. The process for creating section subpages is exactly the same as creating any other page on the Open Atrium site. The only exception is that we change the **Parent Item** in the drop-down selection when we create the page. In our example, we are going to create two subpages under the section **Leave** and then another subpage under the section **Employee Benefits & Awards**.

From the current page we are currently viewing on in the **Notebook** section, we can choose **Add child page** just like we did before.

After adding the three new pages our table of contents will look like the following screenshot:

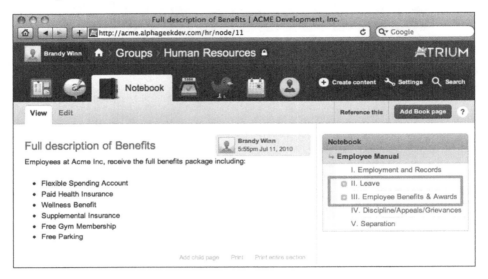

As you can see, the icon to the left of the documents with subsections has changed to a plus symbol indicating that there are additional documents in this section. Clicking on the plus symbol will expand the table of contents to reveal the subpages in a particular section as shown in the following screenshot:

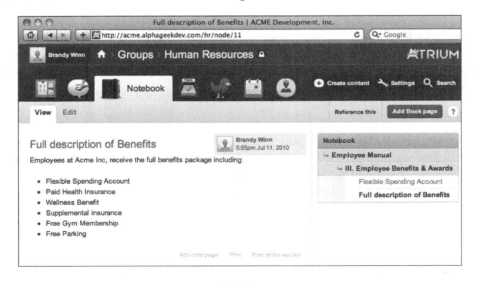

Attachments

The next feature when creating documents in the Notebook is the ability to add attachments to any of the documents. This allows us to use existing documents that may be images or that were created in other formats such as the following:

- Word Processing Documents (DOC)
- Spreadsheet Documents (XLS)
- Portable Document Format (PDF)
- Images (JPG, PNG)
- Design Files (PSD)

One example of attaching documents would be a Human Resources benefit form that has to be filled out by employees, signed, and turned back in. Many benefit providers will provide PDF versions of these forms. We can then upload the PDFs with the appropriate benefit or policy document in the manual.

To attach a file, we can create a new document or can edit an existing document and find the **Attach files to this _____ page**, where the blank is filled in by the type of document you are reviewing. The following screenshot shows an example of what the **Attach files to this** section looks like:

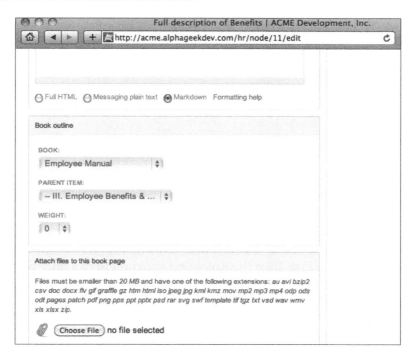

Here we see the familiar **Choose File** button that we see throughout many different websites and allow us to upload content. We can click on **Choose File** and locate a file on our computer to upload and attach to this document. Once we have selected a file, the file will be uploaded and associated with our document. As we can see in the following screenshot, we have the option to **List, Remove, Rename** or **Delete** the file:

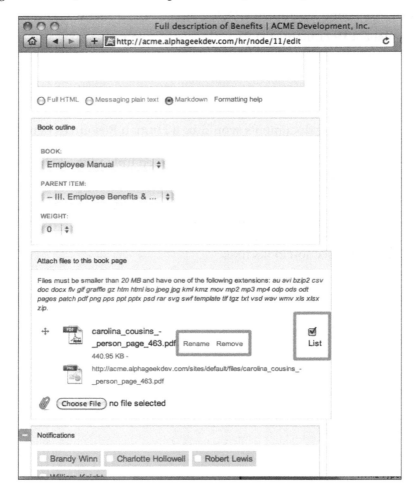

Listing the file allows the uploaded attachment to be displayed when viewing the document. If we uncheck **List**, then the uploaded attachment can only be accessed by people with edit rights to the document. This may be useful for attaching supporting documentation that should not necessarily be displayed with the document. However, it is helpful to have it attached, so that an administrator can quickly access the document. By clicking on the **Remove** link, the uploaded attachment will be unassociated and removed from our system when the document is saved.

Now when we view the document after saving, we will see the uploaded attachment along with a corresponding icon that matches the extension of the document uploaded, if one is available. In our example, we uploaded the `flexible_spending_application.pdf` file and now when we view the document it looks like the following:

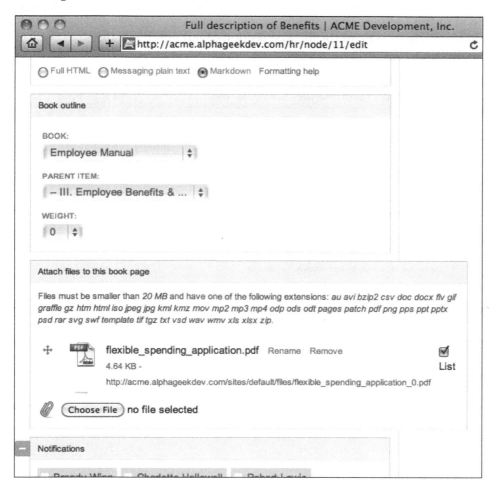

In this section we learned how to create, edit, and attach documents to a book or Notebook content item. The employee manual example is just one example of the many different uses for creating book pages. Other examples could include monthly/quarterly reports, meeting minutes for a particular project, or client presentations.

Printing book pages

There are two options available when it comes to printing book pages. We can click on **Print** on any given page, which will give us a nicely formatted page with a header and footer, the author, and the date on which the document was last edited. The **Print** link is located at the bottom of the document between **Add child page** and **Print entire section**. The following screenshot is an example of what you will see when you click on **Print** for the first section of our employee manual, Section I, Employment and Records:

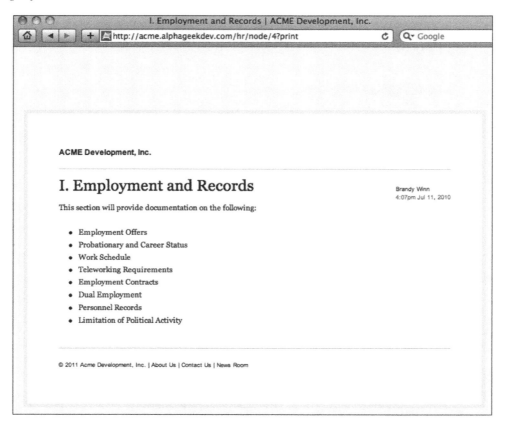

The next option is the ability to print out the entire section using the **Print entire section** link at the bottom of a particular document. This will print out all the documents contained in the section. The following image shows an example of the entire section printed from Section III, Employee Benefits & Awards:

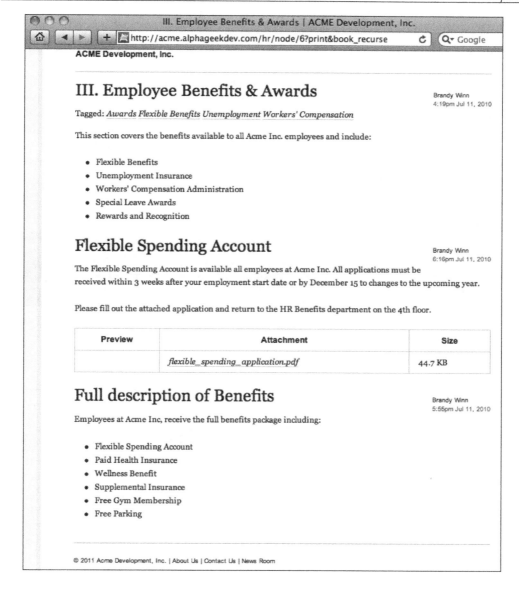

ACME Development, Inc.

III. Employee Benefits & Awards

Brandy Winn
4:19pm Jul 11, 2010

Tagged: *Awards Flexible Benefits Unemployment Workers' Compensation*

This section covers the benefits available to all Acme Inc. employees and include:

- Flexible Benefits
- Unemployment Insurance
- Workers' Compensation Administration
- Special Leave Awards
- Rewards and Recognition

Flexible Spending Account

Brandy Winn
6:16pm Jul 11, 2010

The Flexible Spending Account is available all employees at Acme Inc. All applications must be received within 3 weeks after your employment start date or by December 15 to changes to the upcoming year.

Please fill out the attached application and return to the HR Benefits department on the 4th floor.

Preview	Attachment	Size
	flexible_spending_application.pdf	44.7 KB

Full description of Benefits

Brandy Winn
5:55pm Jul 11, 2010

Employees at Acme Inc, receive the full benefits package including:

- Flexible Spending Account
- Paid Health Insurance
- Wellness Benefit
- Supplemental Insurance
- Free Gym Membership
- Free Parking

© 2011 Acme Development, Inc. | About Us | Contact Us | News Room

Both of these print options can come in handy when it's necessary to print out a copy of a particular section or an entire section to take to a meeting for further discussion. We can also click on the **Employee Manual** document, which is the highest level document in our example, and click on **Print entire section**, which will print out the whole manual.

Archived Notebooks

If a book or Notebook has outlived its usefulness, but we still want to keep it available for future reference, we can choose to archive the Notebook. To view archived notebooks, we can click on the **Archived** tab from the Notebook's main page. Only the entire book can be archived, not individual book pages. To archive a book, click on the book's main page and then click on **Archive**. On the confirmation screen, we click on **Archive**. This will archive the book and also prevent the content from being altered. We can also reactivate the book if we decide that this book should not be archived or we need to alter the content. The following is a screenshot of the **Archived** tab on the **Notebook** page:

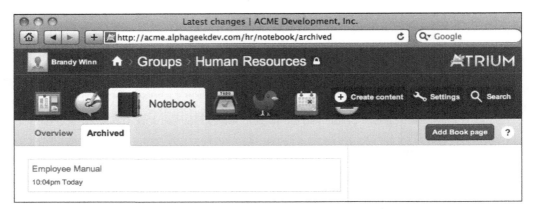

Reference this via Blog entry

On the top menu bar on the same line as the **View**, **Edit**, **Archive** options, there is an option named **Reference this**. It allows us to associate this content with other pages on our site. In an earlier example while discussing revisions, we modified the **V. Separation** section to include a **Termination and Notice** document. While viewing this page, we can click on **Reference this** and select **via Blog entry** to blog about this particular item and create a link back to this document. The following screenshot shows the position of **Reference this** with the **via Blog entry** displayed:

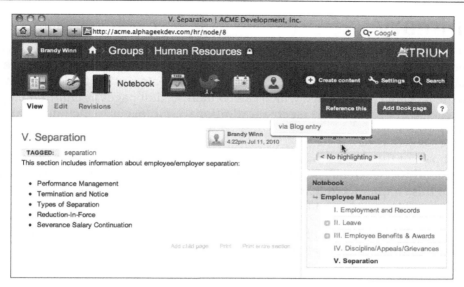

Clicking on the **via Blog Entry** will take us to the **Create blog entry** page where we can enter the title, body, and keywords, similar to any other content page. The difference is that this page will have a new section on it named **Reference page** which will contain a pointer back to the original document. This uses a contributed module "Node Reference" available on Drupal.org, and comes preinstalled with the Open Atrium installation. The following screenshot is an example of the **Referenced page** section:

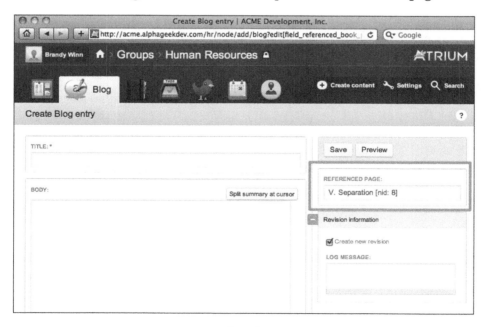

Summary

In this chapter, we learned how to create Notebook or book pages. These pages can be used for manuals, policies, wiki pages, or almost anything else where we need to maintain some type of hierarchical structure. In the create section we learned that we can create a primary book page which can contain section pages as children pages. Within each section page, we can create additional child pages to include documents in each section.

The next part of the chapter will walk through viewing content changes between revisions and will teach us how to print out all or part of a section page. The final section of this chapter looked at uploading attachments to pages and referencing documents in blog posts, and how to archive notebooks.

In the following chapter, *Chapter 8, Blogs*, we will take a closer look at the blog entry page and creating a blog or set of blogs on our Open Atrium site.

8
Blogs

In this chapter, we cover an important feature in Open Atrium, called the blog. The blog in Open Atrium allows each group, or a department, to create a blog entry to be accessed from the dashboard. Blog entries are similar in structure to the Notebook/ Document Library content items and at a minimum include the title and body fields. The blog feature can be used by departments as a way to communicate informally to members of their department. When setting up a blog a user has the option to allow comments. Blog entries and comments can have files attached to them as well. An example of a blog entry for Acme Inc. could include the case where the HR Administrator needed to communicate changes to a policy that was created in *Chapter 7*. When creating the blog entry, the HR Administrator will have the option to reference the policy previously created and attach it to the blog entry.

In this chapter we will learn how to:

- Enable the blog feature
- Create a new blog entry
- Attach a file to a blog entry
- Edit a blog entry
- Add and reply to comments

Enabling the blog feature

To enable the blog feature on a particular department or group page, we will need to be logged in as a manager or admin for a particular group, and go to their dashboard and click on the **Settings** button at the upper-right corner. The following screenshot shows where the **Settings** button is located on the Human Resources department dashboard:

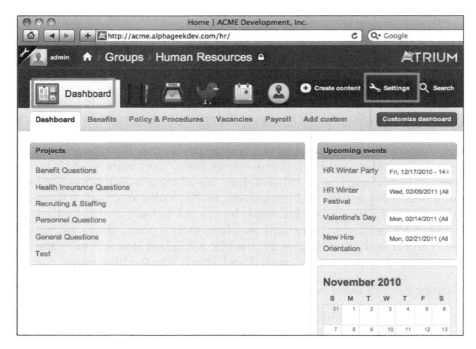

When we click on the **Settings** button, we will see a drop-down menu. In the drop-down menu, select **Customize features** as shown in the following screenshot:

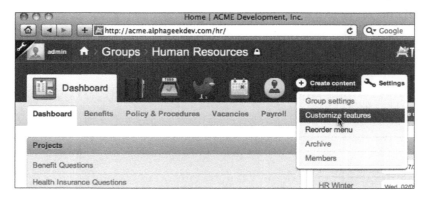

Clicking on **Customize features** will take us to the **Features** tab for the Human
Resources settings page. Here we can enable and disable specific features for the
department's Open Atrium section. For now, we will choose to enable the **Atrium
Blog** by selecting **Enabled** in the drop-down next to **Atrium Blog**, as shown in the
following screenshot:

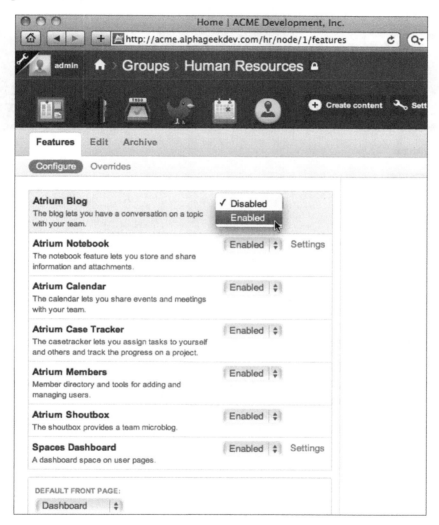

Then we will click on **Save for Human Resources** at the bottom of the form. We should then notice a new icon appear on the top menu bar. The following screenshot shows what the new icon looks like for the blog:

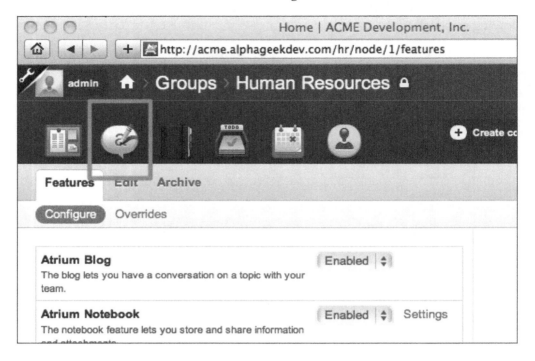

Creating a new blog entry

When we first click on the **Blog** icon, we will see a screen that prompts us to add our first blog entry. The **Add Blog entry** button will always appear on the top right just below the menu bar when we are on the blog page. This button can be used to create new blog posts after the first blog entry button disappears. The following screenshot is an example of the blog entry screen that appears just after clicking on the blog icon:

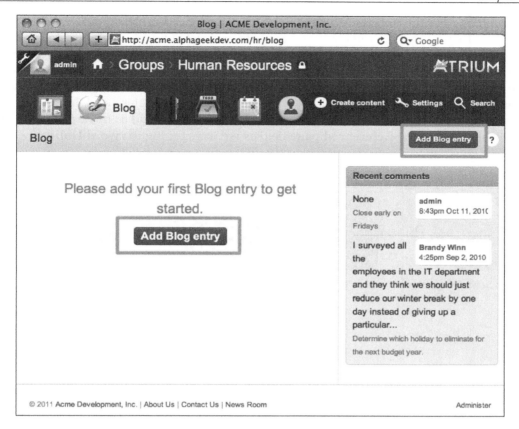

Clicking on **Add Blog entry** in either the top right or the middle of the page will take us to the **Create Blog entry** page. This page should look familiar as it is very similar to other content entry pages in Drupal and Open Atrium. For this example, we are going to create a blog entry about the updated holiday leave policy. The following are the key items that we will use on this page:

- **Title**: Updated Holiday Leave Policy
- **Body**: The Holiday Leave policy for ACME, Inc. has been updated to include all the official holidays for the company. Please refer to this new policy found in the employee manual notebook.
- **Referenced Page**: Holiday Leave [nid:9]
- **Log Message**: First revision of Holiday Leave Blog Entry

We will go ahead and fill our form with the preceding information.

When filling out the **Referenced page** field, we simply need to start typing the title of the page that we want to reference and the auto complete widget will locate the correct page for us. In this example, we started typing **Holida** and the auto complete widget found **Holiday Leave**, which was the exact document we wanted to reference. Once we have selected **Holiday Leave**, the title is then placed in the **Referenced page** field along with an identifier that points back to the the page being referenced. In Drupal, this identifier is known as the **node id** or **nid**. In this case, the **nid** is 9. The following screenshot shows the **Referenced page** field as we were typing the word **Holida**:

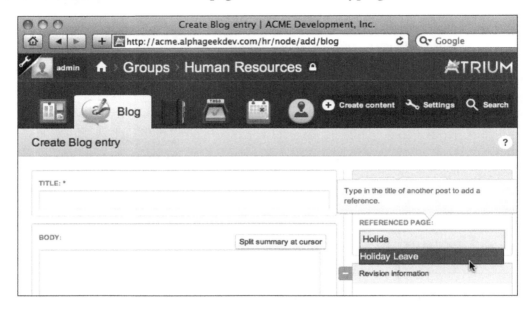

Once all the fields are filled out we can click on the **Preview** button to see what the blog entry will look like, or we can click on the **Save** button to save the new blog entry. For now, we will click on **Preview** to see what the blog entry will look like before saving. This also provides us with another opportunity to edit any fields before we initially save the blog entry. The following image shows our **Updated Holiday Leave Policy** blog entry in a **Preview** mode:

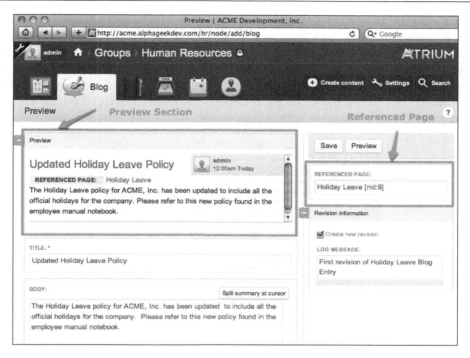

We can then click on **Save** in the upper right-hand corner and we should then see the **View Page** for this blog entry.

Note: There are a couple of additional fields that are hidden by default on some of the forms, including the blog entry form. This keeps the forms simple for initial learning of Open Atrium. In some cases, we will want to add the following set of fields to be displayed on our form.

- **Authoring information**
- **Publishing options**
- **Comment settings**

We can add these fields by going to **Administer | Content Management | Content Types | Blog Entry | Manage Fields**. Here we will have the option to uncheck **hide** by certain field sets. We will go into more detail on how to do this in *Chapter 11, Customization*.

By clicking on the **Blog** icon and then clicking on the **Updated Holiday Leave Policy** title, we will go to the View page, which adds additional fields for posting comments, configuring notifications, and attaching files. Options are also included to print and to close the comment thread. By closing the comment thread, we will retain any existing comments for a particular entry while preventing new comments from being entered. The following screenshot depicts a portion of what the blog view page looks like when logged in with admin privileges:

Clicking on the **Referenced page** link will take us directly to the **Holiday Leave** page in our employee manual. We will see a new section that appears on the Holiday Leave page and shows what other pages also reference this page. The following screenshot shows an example of the **Holiday Leave** policy after adding our first blog entry and referencing this page:

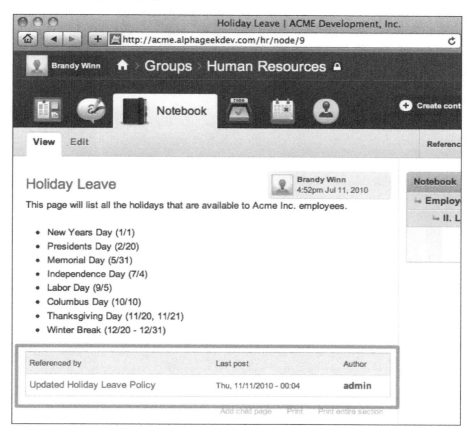

Attaching a file to a blog entry

Now, suppose we want our users to be able to quickly print out a PDF of the **Holiday Leave** policy. The first thing we would do is create a PDF of our policy to be attached to our blog entry. For this example, we can use any PDF file to demonstrate how to attach it to the blog entry. Once we have a PDF file, we can click on the **Blog** icon to view our entries and click on the title of the blog entry. Now, we can click on the **Edit** link and scroll down to the **Attach files to this blog entry section**.

The following screenshot shows an example of the **Attach files** section:

Now, we click on **Choose File** and locate the PDF file that we want to attach. Once we have selected the file in the file browser window, it will be automatically uploaded. A progress bar will show briefly while the document is being uploaded and then we will see the file listed in the **Attach files** section, as shown in the following screenshot:

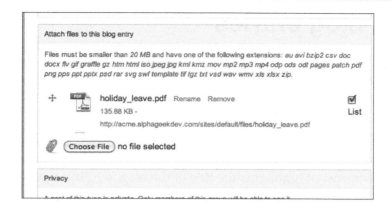

Then we need to click on **Save** in the upper-right corner to ensure that our newly attached PDF file is attached with our document. After clicking on **Save**, we should return to the view screen of our blog entry and see our PDF file attached.

A portion of the view screen for our updated holiday leave policy is shown in the following screenshot where we can see the PDF file attached to our blog entry:

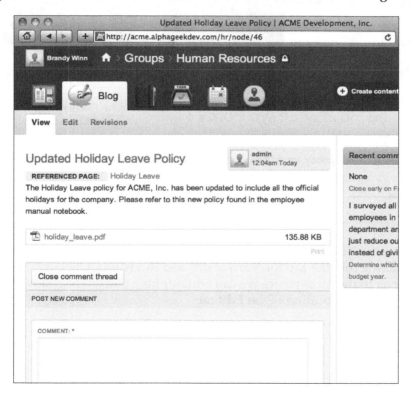

Editing blog entries

Editing a blog entry is very similar to editing any other piece of content in Drupal or Open Atrium. Editing a blog entry uses the same form that we used to create our blog entry. So far we have created one blog entry. By clicking on the **Blog** icon on the menu bar, we can view the most recent blog entries. Even though we can see our blog entry, we do not have a way of editing the entry from this screen. To edit the blog entry we can click on the title of the blog to view the full version of the entry. Here we will see the **Edit** tab. If a particular user did not create the blog entry and does not have administrator rights, he/she will not be able to see the **Edit** option. The following screenshot highlights the title of the blog, which is where we need to click to be able to edit the blog entry:

By clicking on the **Title**, we will then see a form that allows us to add comments along with tabs across the top for **View**, **Edit**, and **Revisions**. Clicking on the **Edit** tab will take us to the form where we can edit our blog entry. The following screenshot shows the location of the **Edit** tab:

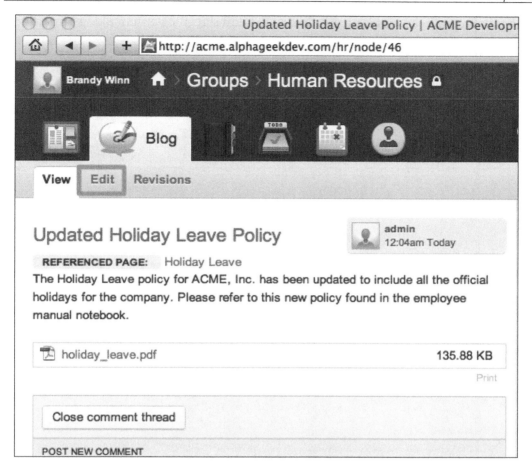

After clicking on **Edit**, we will see the blog entry with our information in the fields and can now make our edits to the form. For this blog entry, we are going to make a couple of edits and add some additional text to the **Body field**.

The following screenshot is an example of the edit screen prior to making our edits:

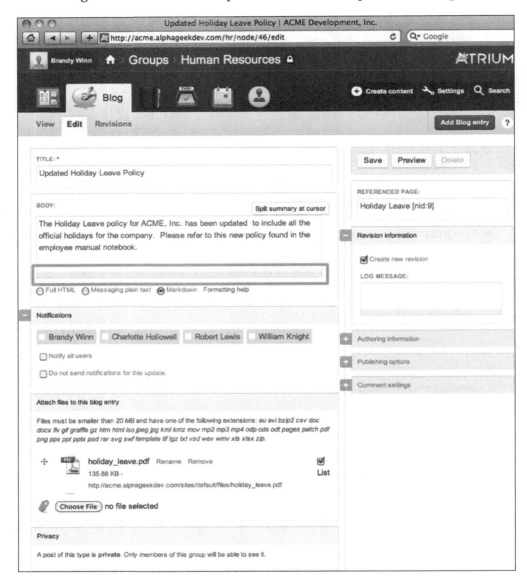

Under the **Revision information** section on the right-hand sidebar, we will leave **Create new revision** checked and then add a **Log message**. This will provide a reference note that we can use while reviewing revisions.

For this blog entry, we are going to make a couple of edits. We are going to add the following additional text to the **Body** field, and remove the file attachment:

- **Body**: This policy is currently under review, and will be updated as changes are made to the official policy.

- **Log Message**: Added additional text to body field and removed file attachment

- **Remove file attachment**: To remove the file attachment, click on the **Remove** link next to the attachment.

The following screenshot shows our blog edit screen after our changes have been made:

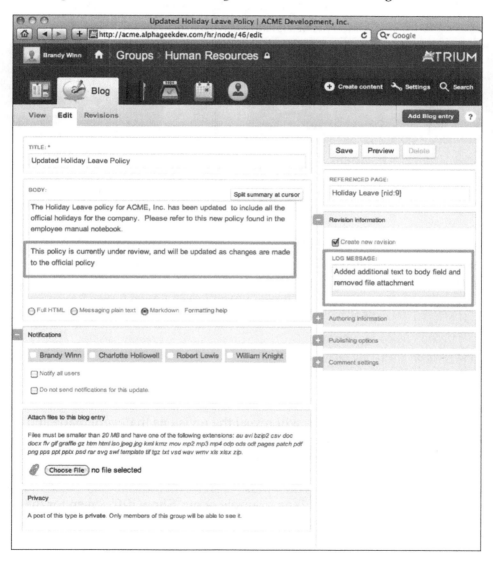

Once we have verified that the information we added is correct, we can click on **Save**.

Revisions

As we discussed earlier, the **Revisions** tab will show all the revisions for a particular content item. We can see from the following screenshot that our recent edits have created a new revision, which is labeled **current revision**:

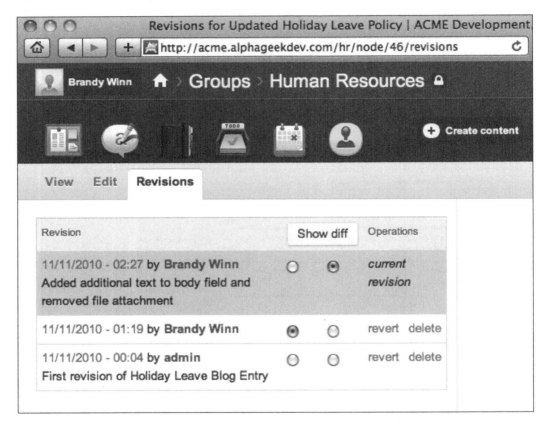

Clicking on the **Show diff** button will reveal the revisions that were made and highlight the changes. The revisions will be displayed in two columns. The left-hand column will contain the oldest revision and the right-hand column will contain the newer revision. Any item with a minus (-) sign will indicate that the item was changed or removed. Any item with a plus (+) sign will indicate that the item was added. The following screenshot is an example of our **Show diff** screen for the two most recent revisions to our blog entry:

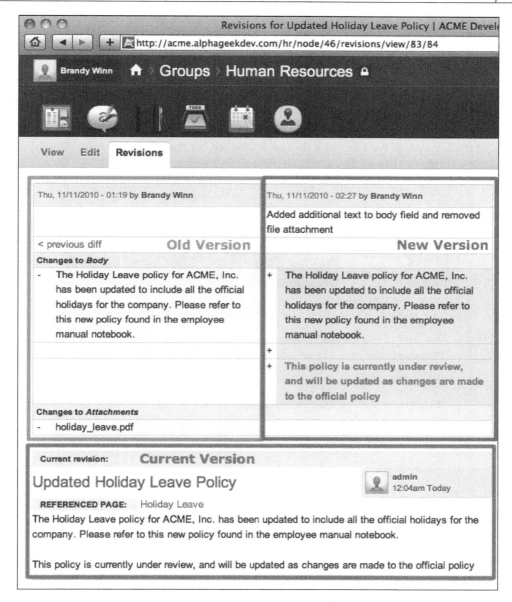

In the case of the most recent revision, all the body text is marked as being removed, and then the first paragraph is marked as being added. The text that changed between the two is marked in red text. We will also see that the left-hand column contains a minus sign next to **holiday_leave.pdf** indicating that we removed the file attachment. There is nothing in the right-hand column next to this because we did not replace the attachments.

Commenting

One of the key differences between the blog content type and the Notebook/ Document Library is that blogs can have comments associated with them. This allows a department to open up topics for a threaded discussion based on the blog entry. As an author of a blog entry or an administrator, we have the option of closing the comment thread at any time. This allows controlling the flow of comments by preventing new comments from being entered. To close the commenting for a particular blog entry, we can click on the **View** tab for the blog entry and then click on **Close comment thread** as shown in the following screenshot:

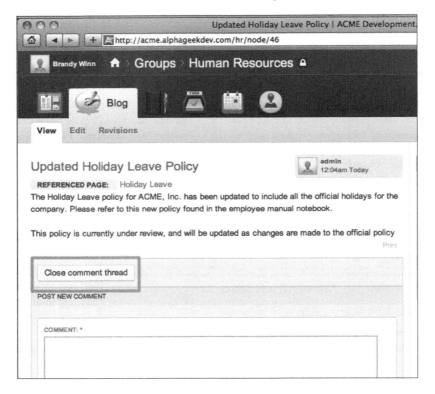

Prior to closing the comment thread, we can add a new comment from this page, or click on the main **Blog** tab, and under a particular blog entry click on **Add new comment**. As soon as we click on the **Add new comment** tab, we will have the option to add our comment text, select notifications, and add file attachments related to this comment. We can type in our comment and then click on **Save.** After clicking on **Save**, the comment will be added to the comment thread. If someone were to leave an inappropriate comment or a comment that was questionable, any administrator can edit the comment as well as the original poster. The following screenshot shows our updated holiday leave policy blog entry with three comments added:

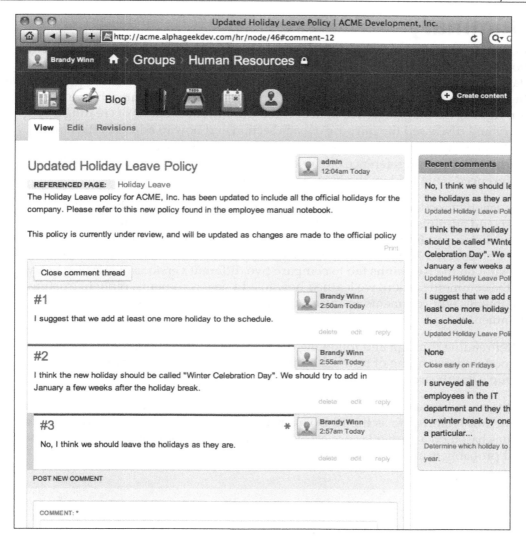

We can see that the third comment is indented slightly to indicate that it is in reply to the second comment. Also, worth noting is that you can see the **Recent comments** column, which contains the three comments that are just added.

Summary

In this chapter, we learned how to add the blog feature to a group or department's home page by enabling it in Open Atrium. This added a new icon on our group dashboard page for viewing and creating blog entries. Anyone in the department can then contribute to the group blog by clicking on the **Add blog entry** button on the top right of the blog page. We then covered the various sections of creating a blog entry and discussed the purpose of each section and how to add file attachments to the blog entry for associating additional content with each blog entry. We also learned that we can reference other non-blog content on our site by using the **Referenced page** field on the blog entry screen.

The last two sections of this chapter covered how to edit existing blog entries, post, and administer comments. We learned that by clicking on the blog title and then clicking on **Edit**, we can change any of the existing fields on our blog entry. We also covered how to add log messages and compare revisions. We did this by clicking on the **Revisions** tab to compare two different versions of our blog entry. In the comment section, we learned how to add new comments, reply to existing comments, edit comments as an administrator, and how to close a particular comment thread.

After reading through and following the examples in this chapter, you should have a good understanding of how useful the blog feature can be on your department's or group's dashboards.

In the next chapter, we will go through examples of the Case Tracker feature, sometimes referred to as the To Do list feature. This feature allows us to add cases or issues based on a particular project. This feature can be used in many different ways, and probably is used mostly as a bug tracking feature.

9
Case Tracker

In this chapter, we will learn how to use the **Case Tracker** feature of Open Atrium. The **Case Tracker** feature is similar to other issue tracking applications that you may be familiar with. This feature allows us to separate tasks and issues into separate projects and assign priorities and statuses to each item. It also hooks into the commenting module built into Drupal to allow users to add comments as the life cycle of the issue progresses.

This chapter will cover the following topics:

- Anatomy of a bug/issue
- Enabling the Case Tracker feature
- Creating projects
- Entering cases
- Finding cases
- Managing projects
- Viewing cases

Many of the items used with the Case Tracker feature are very similar to the blog and Notebook features discussed in previous chapters. The Case Tracker feature includes additional features tailored specifically for tracking issues.

This feature is flexible enough for different departments to use the Case Tracker in different ways. For example, the Information Technology department may use the Case Tracker for tracking IT support requests while the Human Resources department may use the Case Tracker to track inquires about benefits, policies, and recruiting. To demonstrate this feature, we will continue using the Human Resources department as an example.

Throughout this chapter, we may refer to cases in several different ways. An organization might have specific terminology to refer to cases. In this chapter, all of these terms refer back to what Open Atriums calls a case:

- Case
- Bug
- Ticket
- Issue

Anatomy of a bug

Before we dive into creating projects and cases, it is important to understand how bug/issue tracking systems are constructed. Each issue has a finite start point and end point. In between the start and end points, there may be communication between the report of the bug and the person assigned to work on the bug. This communication is usually to gather more information or make notes about potential solutions to the problem being addressed. There are many different types of bug tracking programs available; some are Open Source, such as Open Atrium, while others may charge a flat fee or monthly fee to use a particular system. Some of the more popular bug tracking programs include the following:

- Bugzilla: `http://www.bugzilla.org`
- Unfuddle: `http://unfuddle.com/`
- JIRA: `http://www.atlassian.com/software/jira/`
- FogBugz: `http://fogcreek.com/FogBugz/`
- Trac: `http://trac.edgewall.org/`

There are many other bug tracking programs available that you can find simply by searching for bug tracking through your favorite search engine. Your organization or company may have a corporate implementation of one of these systems, in which case you may not need the Case Tracker features in Open Atrium.

The main anatomy of a bug includes fields to track the following:

- Priority
- Status
- Assigned to
- Description
- Reporter

These fields ensure that all of the necessary information can be referenced when addressing an issue. Status is an important field when tracking issues, as it tells the viewer exactly what state the issue is in. Bugs go through several different states or statuses in their life cycle. Typical status include the following:

- New
- Assigned
- Resolved
- Reopened
- Verified
- Closed

Of course, each bug tracking program may differ depending on the types of statuses used or what they are called, but for the most part, a bug follows the following pattern:

- **Open**: New issue created
- **Assigned**: Who will work on the bug
- **Fixed**: Bug has been fixed or question has been answered
- **Verified**: The report or a quality control person determines that the solution is acceptable
- **Closed**: The bug has been completed

The following diagram shows the typical life cycle of a bug:

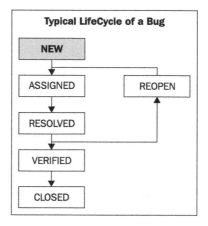

Enabling the Case Tracker feature

To enable the Case Tracker feature on a particular department or group's page, we will need to be logged in as an administrator for a particular group, and from the dashboard click on **Settings** at the upper right of the screen. This will provide a drop-down menu where we can then click on **Customize features**. The following screenshot shows where the **Settings** button is located on the Human Resources department dashboard:

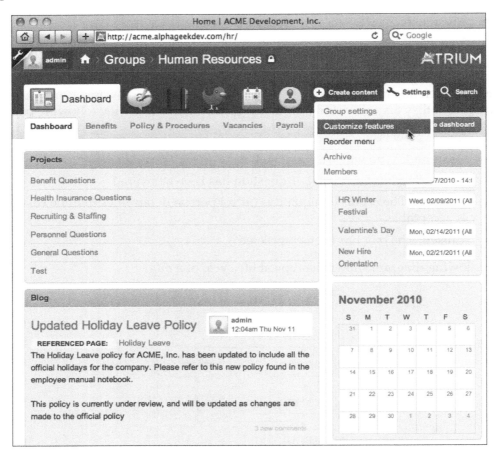

After clicking on **Customize features** in the settings menu, a list of all the available features will be displayed in the first tab. Here we have the ability to enable and disable specific features. Locate the Atrium **Case Tracker** feature and change the drop-down selection from **Disabled** to **Enabled**. In the following screenshot, we can see that the **Atrium Case Tracker** option is the fourth item in the list:

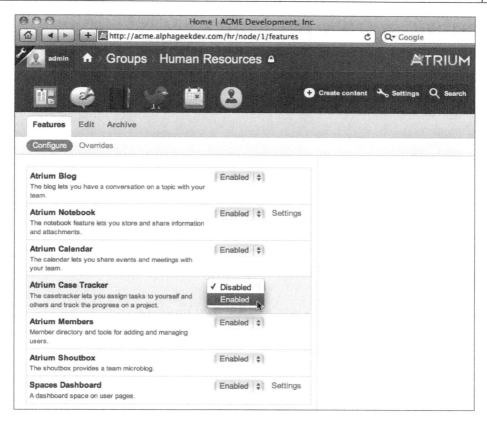

After selecting **Enabled** for **Atrium Case Tracker**, scroll down to the bottom of the screen and click on the **Save for Human Resources** button to ensure that the Case Tracker feature is enabled. If everything is saved correctly, we should now see a Case Tracker icon on our toolbar as indicated in the following screenshot:

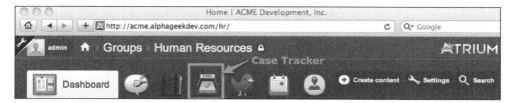

At this point, we have now enabled the Case Tracker feature for the Human Resources group. To enable the Case Tracker feature for other groups or departments, we will go through the same steps from each of the group's Dashboard pages.

Creating a new project

Cases are organized by projects that must be created prior to entering a case. A project categorizes different types of cases into groups. For example, the IT department might create several projects that include the following:

- Server architecture
- Help desk
- Website
- Software development

To add a new case, we will first need to add a new project. Each project created can contain a different set of related cases. As we learned earlier, each department or group can have a unique set of projects. This provides the ability for each department to customize and maintain issues separately from other groups. To create a new project, click on the **Case Tracker** tab and then click on **Add project** located at the upper right corner.

The following screenshot is an example of the **Add Project** screen:

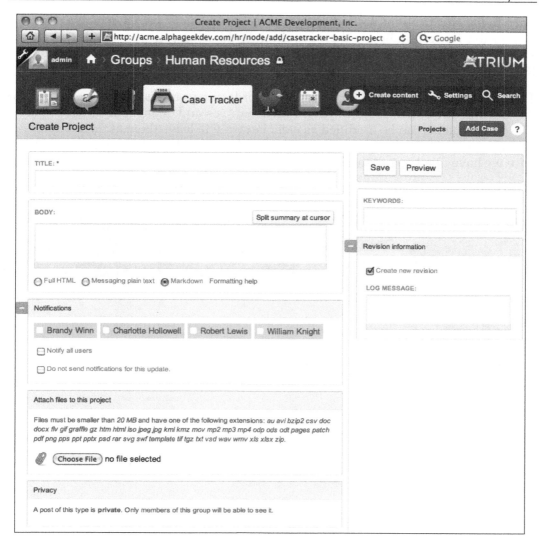

This form is similar in structure to the other features that we have worked with in previous chapters. To demonstrate creating a project, we will create a project for the Human Resources department to track benefit inquiries.

We will start by filling out the content fields on the page. For the **Title** field, we will use `Benefit Questions` and for the **Body** field, we will include a short description of the project.

Then in the **Notifications** section, we will select the primary people who will be responsible for responding to these inquiries. In this example, we will select `Brandy Winn` to be notified, as she will be tracking all the incoming issues for the Human Resources department.

Then for **Keywords**, we will type a few keywords or tags to assist when searching for this document. For this project, we will use `Benefits` and `Questions` as keywords. The other sections can be modified as well, but we will leave them at their default settings for now. The Create Project screen will look like the following screenshot once we have filled out all the fields:

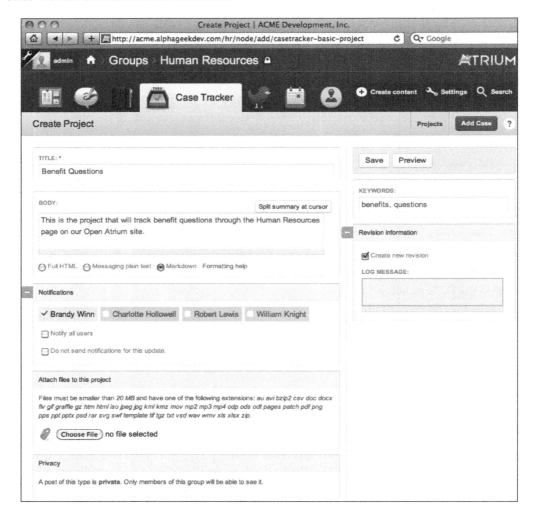

Now we can click on **Save** and our first project will be created.

Entering new cases

Now that we have created our first project, we can begin adding cases. First we will want to log out as the admin user and log in as a normal user who is a part of the Human Resources group. In this example, we will log in as Charlotte Hollowell. Charlotte has a question about whether her insurance benefits cover the cost of over-the-counter reading glasses.

To log out, click on the username at the top-left corner of the screen and then click on **Log out**. Now click on the **Log in** button on the top left and enter the username and password for Charlotte Hollowell and click on **Log in**. Navigate to the Human Resources dashboard, which can be located by typing **/hr** after the site name. Now click on the **Case Tracker** (ToDo) icon on the menu bar. This will change the focus of the Dashboard to the Case Tracker screens.

Now to add a case, we can click on the **Add case** button located on the top-right of the Case Tracker screen as shown in the following screenshot:

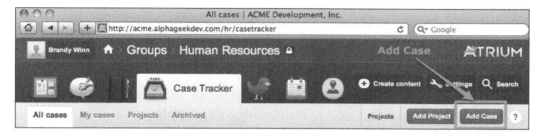

This will bring up the **Create Case** form which is similar in structure to other forms throughout the Open Atrium system. In the Case Tracker feature, the **Add case** form contains an additional section named **Case information**, which contains specific fields for tracking cases.

Add case field descriptions

This section will provide an explanation of each field on the **Add case** form.

Title

The first field that we will enter is the **Title** field. The **Title** field can be used as a short description or summary about the issue.

Case information

The next field on the form is the **Case information** field. Here we will select the project that this issue belongs to, choose a person to assign the issue to, and set the status, priority, and type fields.

Project

If you have created more than one project, then a drop-down will allow us to select which project we want to enter this case in. If there is only one project, then the case will automatically be entered for the existing project.

Assign to

The **Assign to** section allows us to assign the case directly to a particular HR staff member. For this example, we will assign this case to Unassigned because we are not sure who should be addressing this issue.

Status

Status allows us to specify what state the issue is in as the case goes through the typical life cycle.

The default statuses include the following:

- **Open**: The open status indicates that the bug has not been fixed and may either be in a waiting state to be fixed, or a fix is in progress.
- **Resolved**: The resolved status is used to signify that the issue or problem has been fixed and is complete. In the case of a software patch, the resolved status would indicate that it is to be tested and verified. In the case of a question or answer, it may indicate that the issue has been answered.
- **Deferred**: The deferred status states that the issue is not ready to be addressed at this point in time and will be addressed later.
- **Duplicate**: The duplicate status indicates that the issue has already been reported and is being tracked as a separate issue.
- **Closed**: The closed status indicates that the issue has been verified and fixed.

Priority

Priority is a flag field to indicate how urgently this issue or case needs to be addressed. The default priorities are:

- High
- Normal
- Low

An issue marked with a **High** priority means that the issue should be addressed as soon as possible before any other issue. A **Normal** priority means that the matter is not urgent and can wait until other more pressing issues have been addressed. Finally, a **Low** priority issue is usually considered a "nice to have" item, and should not be addressed until after all higher priority items have been addressed. In some cases, a **Low** priority item may be an easy fix or an easy question to answer, in which case, it may make sense to go ahead and resolve that issue quickly to reduce the total number of open items.

Type

Type classifies the bug in a particular category. The types included with the default Open Atrium installation include:

- Bug
- Feature request
- General task

To change the default status, type, or priority, you can navigate to the **Case settings** page at http://www.example.com/admin/settings/casetracker/states. Here you can edit and delete each of the items to more closely match your company's terminology.

Body

The **Body** field is used to provide a detailed description of the issue or case. It should include as much detail as possible, so that the person assigned the issue can clearly understand or reproduce the problem. The types of information collected in this field may vary between our groups. In the case of an HR issue tracking system, the **Body** field may contain a textual description of the question, while an IT issue tracking system may contain specific details and steps to replicate a particular problem.

Notifications

The **Notifications** box allows us to select specific users to be notified when this case is submitted or updated. We also have a checkbox to **Notify all users** and to not send any notifications for updates.

Attach files to this case

Providing as much detail as possible is important when we are entering a bug. One way to provide even more detail is to include a screenshot or other supporting documentation. The **Attach files this case** allows us to select a file from our computer to be attached to the case.

Privacy

There are no options available in this section because the HR department is a private group.

Keywords

The **Keywords** section allows us to assign specific tags or categories to our issue. This will help while indexing the site, so that issues marked with a particular tag can be pulled into a result.

Revision information

The last section on the form is the **Revision information** section. This works the same as it does on other forms. It allows us to provide a reference message for the case.

Add case field values

The following fields and values will be used for this case:

Title: HRIS system freezes when I log in.

Project: Benefit Questions

Assign To: Unassigned

Status: Open

Priority: Highest

Type: Bug

Body: Every time I log in to the HRIS system and go to the main menu my screen freezes. If I log in using a different ID everything works fine.

Notifications: Charlotte Hollowell

After the form fields are filled out before clicking on **Save**, our form will look like the following screenshot:

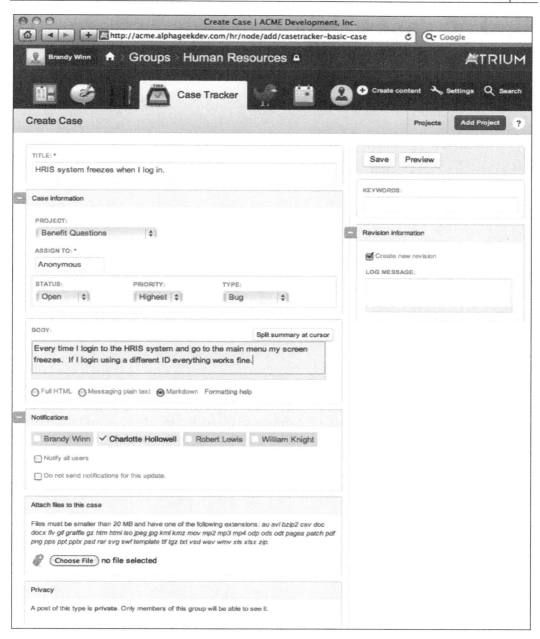

Finding cases

When we first click on the **Case Tracker** icon, we see tabs for the following:

- **All cases**
- **My cases**
- **Projects**
- **Archived**

In the following screenshot, you can see the links to the various sections that we will be discussing in the next few sections:

Viewing cases

The first tab on the Case Tracker screen is the **All cases** tab. The left-hand side of the screen contains list cases. Initially, this list is populated with all of the available cases for our group page. All of the columns can be sorted by clicking on the column header with the exception of the **Title** field. We can toggle the sorting direction for a column by clicking on a column header a second time. We can also filter this list by using the filters located in the right-hand section of the screen under the **Filter results** section. The following screenshot shows the initial view with several cases already entered:

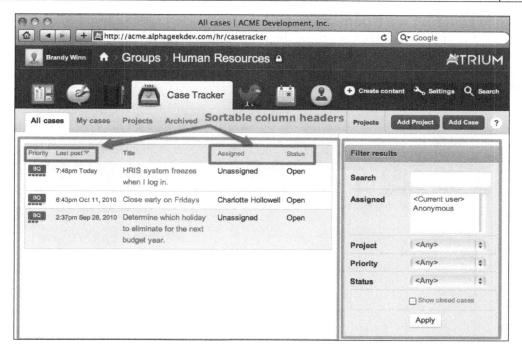

Filtering results

In the preceding screenshot, we can see that the right-hand side of the screen contains the **Filter results** section. These filters allow us to locate a particular case or cases by searching on the following:

- **Search**: Any word in text
- **Assigned**: Whom the case is assigned to
- **Project**: What project a case belongs to
- **Priority**: Priority of the case
- **Status**: Status of the case
- **Show closed cases**: Include closed cases in the search

With this filter, we can type in any text in the search, select specific users who are assigned to an issue, or choose any of the project, priority, and status selections. This will filter the results based on the criteria we entered. The following screenshot shows that the case list is filtered based on the selection of **Brandy Winn** in the **Assigned** field:

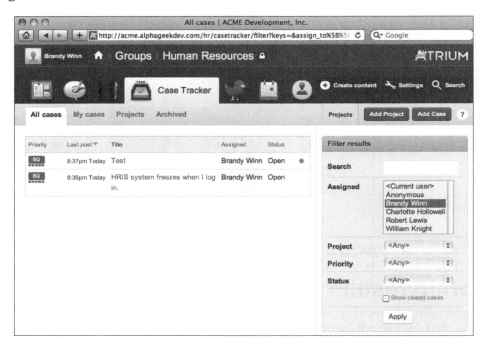

My cases

Just underneath the search filter, you will also see a list of the cases assigned to the currently logged in user. We can also access this list by clicking on **My cases**, which is the second tab from the left on the menu bar under the **Case Tracker** section. This will contain a list of any case that is assigned to the logged in user.

Projects

Clicking on the **Projects** tab provides an overall picture of the various projects that are available. After each project, a summary of the total number of cases will be listed. Projects are a good way to segment Case Tracker issues. In the case of the Human Resources department, we might have the following projects:

- General questions
- Personnel questions
- Recruiting & staffing
- Health insurance questions
- Benefit questions

Earlier in the chapter, we discussed how to create new projects. Let us go ahead and create a project for each of the aforementioned projects and refer back to the **Create new projects** section as needed.

After adding the projects, we can click on the **Case Tracker** icon to return to the Case Tracker dashboard. Now, clicking on the **Projects** tab should provide a summary of all the projects available to our group as shown in the following screenshot:

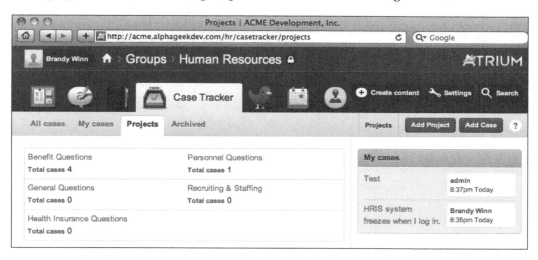

The projects are listed in columnar format with the total number of cases belonging to the project underneath the project name. Now if we click on the **Add case** button, we will see a drop-down menu under **Project** that lists the available projects.

Moving a case between projects

We may find that a case was opened up under the wrong project. In this instance, we will edit the existing case and simply change the project to which it belongs. After clicking on the **Case Tracker** icon, click on the title of any case that we want to edit. This will take us to the case view screen where we can click on the **Edit** tab. Now locate the **Project** field and change the project to an alternate project.

Identifying a project

Open Atrium provides visual indicators on some of the case listings to quickly identify the project and priority of a particular case. To see this, we can return to the **All cases** view by clicking on the **Case Tracker** icon. Each project is given a unique color and a short name that is automatically determined by Open Atrium. Each case is then labeled with an icon in the color for the project and the text for the project abbreviation. Just below the icon there is a graph showing the priority of the case. The more bars listed here the higher the priority. By hovering over the project icon, we can see the full name of the project. The following is a screenshot of what the **All cases** summary screen looks like while hovering over the project icon:

Archiving a project

Often we will want to close a project but not delete it. Deleting a project will remove any cases currently associated with it. The Archive feature allows us to keep a project available as reference, but prevents new cases or comments being added. In the following example, we will archive the Benefit Questions project. First we click on the **Case Tracker** icon and then on the **Projects** tab. Click on the **Benefit Questions** link, and then click on **Archive** as shown in the following screenshot:

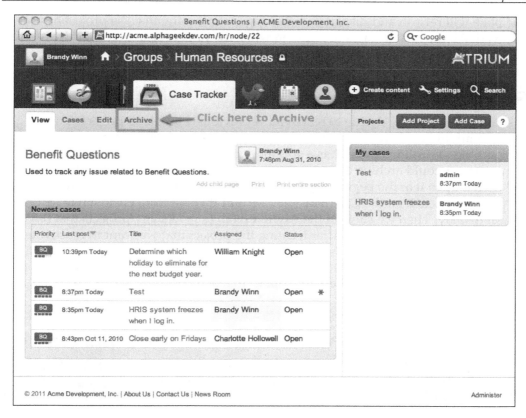

Once we have confirmed that we are in the correct project, we can then click on the **Archive** tab and click on the **Archive** button on the confirmation screen, which looks like the following screenshot:

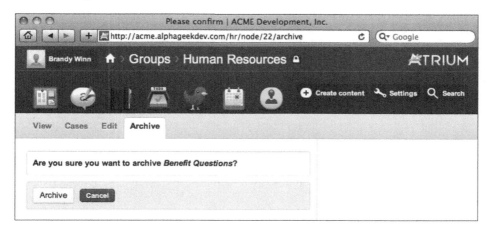

The page will refresh and display two messages confirming that the project has been archived. All the related cases are hidden while the project is archived. However, we can still modify the project title and body.

Reactivation

In some cases, we may decide to reactivate a previously archived project. One example might be where the Human Resources department has a seasonal project, such as Open Enrollment, that has a specific start and end date every year. The HR administrator could archive this project every year when Open Enrollment is closed and then reopen it at the beginning of every Open Enrollment season. To reactivate the project, we click on the **Case Tracker** icon and then on **Projects** to navigate to the project display. Then we click on the **Archived** tab to reveal any projects that have been archived or deactivated. After locating the project that we want to reactivate, we click on its title and locate the **click here** link to reactivate the project. As an alternative, you can click on the **Reactivate** button on the menu bar. The following screenshot is an example of where the link is, to reactivate a project:

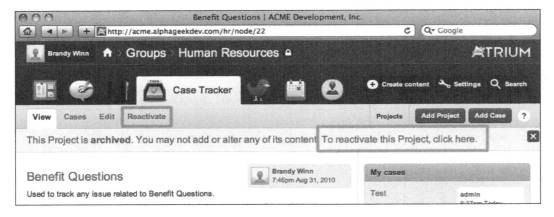

After clicking on the **Reactivate** button or link, we will see a confirmation message to reactivate the project. We can click on the **Reactivate** button and the project will be reactivated. The following is a screenshot of the confirmation message for reactivating a project:

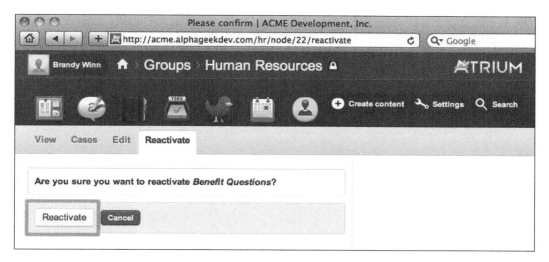

Viewing cases

We have already looked at several cases on the View screen. This section will point out particular areas on the View screen to pay attention to and then walk through the process of adding a comment thread to a case. We can look at any case and in the example provided we will look at the first case in the Benefit Questions project. First, we need to return to the Case Tracker dashboard and click on **Projects** to view the main project screen. Next, we will click on the **Benefit Questions** project. Now, we can select the case we want to view by clicking on the title of the case.

The top half of the View screen for our case is shown in the following screenshot:

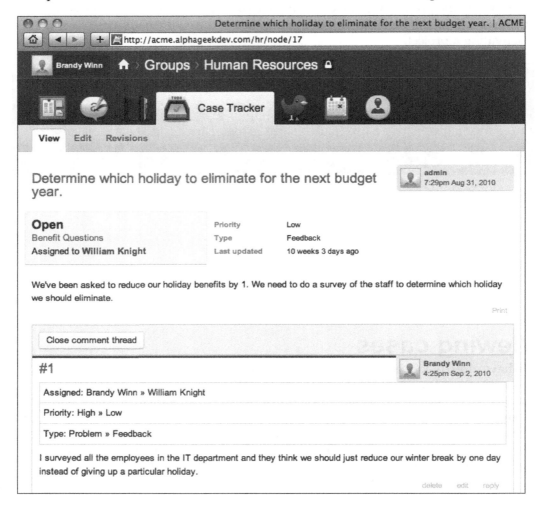

Ticket information

The top half of the ticket includes the status and priority of the cases, as well as the assignee of the ticket, and when it was last updated. It also contains the history behind the ticket, which is also referred to as the comment thread.

Post new comment

The **Post New Comment** section allows us to change the assigned person and edit any of the status, priority, or type options. If the **Case Information** section is not expanded already, we can click the plus sign (+) to expand it. As we edit settings, it is helpful to note in the "comments" an explanation of why we made the changes. To demonstrate posting comments, we will change the assigned person to `Charlotte Hollowell` and modify the priority from low to highest. We will also add a comment explaining this change. The following screenshot shows our comment form just before submitting:

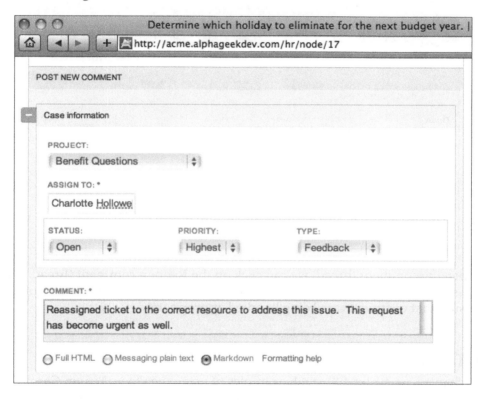

Once we have filled out the comment form, we can add any file attachment and select any notifications and then click on **Save**. Our comment is then added to the audit trail for the issue along with a summary of what was changed.

Close comment thread

At some point before the ticket is closed, we may decide that we no longer want to allow commenting or feedback on the ticket. To close comments, we need to click on the **Close comment thread** button. At this point, no additional comments can be made to the case. To reopen the comment thread, we can click on the **Reopen comment thread** as shown in the following screenshot:

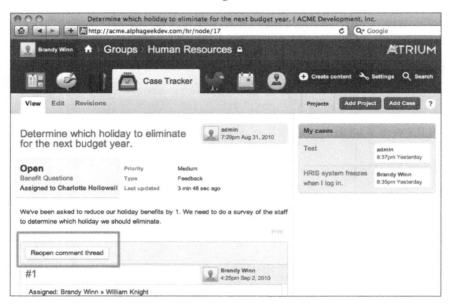

To reopen the comment thread, we can click on the **Reopen comment thread**. This provides the department manager or administrator the ability to moderate comments and ensure that comments are being handled appropriately.

Summary

In this chapter, we walked through examples of using the Open Atrium Case Tracker, also referred to as the To Do list. The first part walked through the life cycle of a bug, including statuses and priorities. Then we covered how to add a new project or category for organizing our cases based on a specific topic or set of topics.

The next couple of sections taught us how to find our cases, and how to manage projects. Finally, in the last section we covered viewing cases and commenting. In the commenting cases section, we learned how to enable and disable comments for a particular case.

In the next chapter, we will explore the Calendar feature of Open Atrium.

10
Calendar

In this chapter, we will cover the Calendar feature in Open Atrium. This feature will allow you to schedule events, and provide calendar feeds in a standard format. It will allow users to subscribe to individual calendars and have events on those calendars downloaded directly into their own calendar application outside of Open Atrium.

In this chapter, we will learn about:

- Enabling the Calendar
- Creating a new event
- Editing an event
- Subscribing to an iCal feed

The next few sections will walk through the different features of the Open Atrium Calendar and provide examples on how to implement and manage the Calendar.

Enabling the Calendar

To enable the Calendar feature, log in as an administrator and navigate to one of the department or group pages. Then click on **Settings** on the menu bar at the upper right. Now click on **Customize features** from the drop-down menu. The following screenshot shows where the **Settings** button is located on the Human Resources department dashboard:

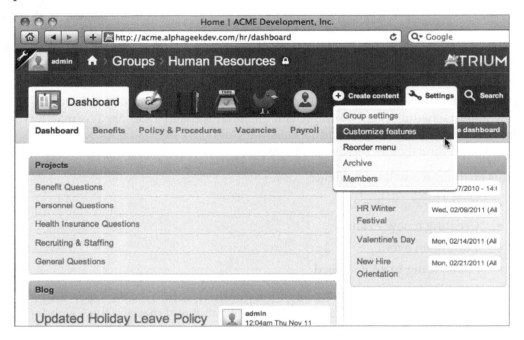

After clicking on **Customize features** in the **Settings** drop-down, we will see a list of all of the available features in the first tab. This is the section where we can enable and disable individual features. Locate the **Atrium Calendar** feature and change the drop-down selection from **Disabled** to **Enabled**. In the following screenshot, we can see that the **Atrium Calendar** option is the third item in the list:

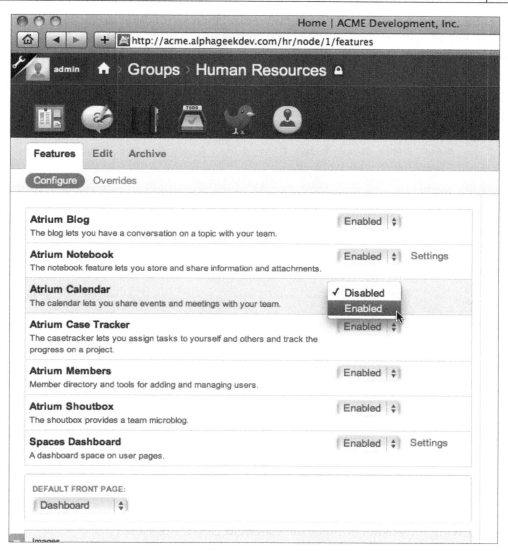

Select **Enabled** for the Atrium Calendar feature, then scroll down to the bottom of the screen and click on the **Save for Human Resources** button to ensure that the Calendar is enabled as indicated in the following screenshot:

If everything is saved correctly, we should now see a **Calendar** icon on our toolbar. The following screenshot outlines the **Calendar** icon for reference:

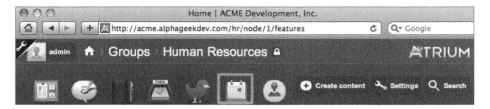

Now we have enabled the Calendar for the Human Resources group. For other departments, we can go through the same steps to enable the Calendar feature.

The Calendar page

Clicking on the **Calendar** icon will take us to the main Calendar page. This page contains the following three tabs:

- Calendar
- Upcoming
- iCal Feeds

Immediately after clicking on the **Calendar** icon, we will be on the main Calendar page. This page shows a full view of the Calendar and provides previous and next links to navigate between past or future months. We can also click on a particular date to bring up the add form to add new events. By default, a list of upcoming events will be listed in the right sidebar. The following screenshot is an example of a Calendar page for February 2011:

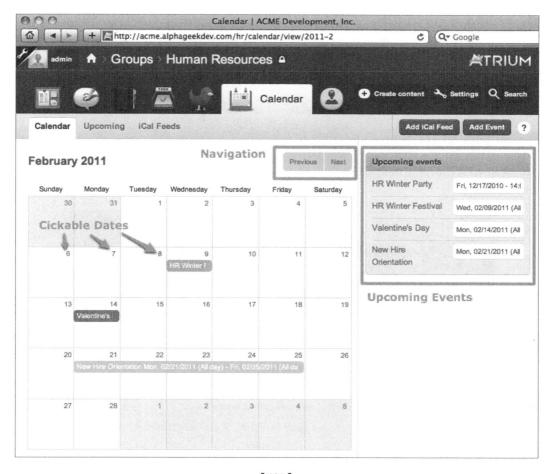

The **Upcoming** tab provides a longer list of all the events that are in the future. We can click on the events title as indicated in the following screenshot to view more details about the event:

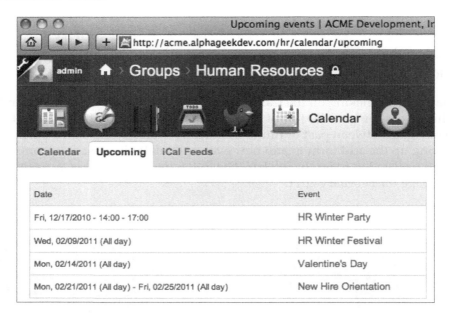

The last tab **iCal Feeds** provides a list of feeds that are currently subscribed to and published in the department Calendar. We will cover how to add iCal Feeds in the last section of this chapter. The following screenshot shows an example of the iCal Feeds listing:

Creating a new event

In this section, we will learn how to create an event to add to our Calendar. Here we can hover over any date and click on **Add** or we can click on the **Add Event** button located on the menu bar to the right. Either option will take us to the Create Event page, which is shown in the following screenshot:

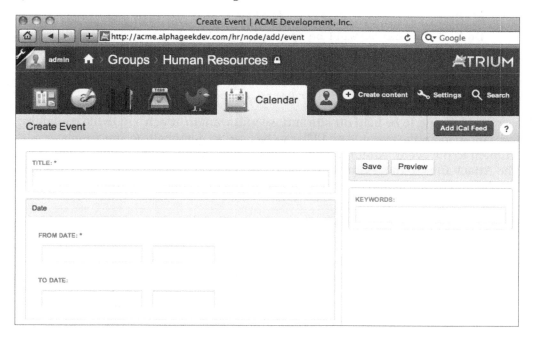

The bottom half of the page is exactly the same as other content entry pages with attachments, notifications, and privacy sections. The main difference between this page and other content entry pages is that there is a **Date** field set, which allows us to specify a From Date and a To Date. The From Date is required for all types of events. The To Date is not required for single date events and is used to mark events that span more than one day. The fields used for the Create Event page are listed below:

- Title
- Date (From Date / To Date)
- Body
- Notifications
- Attach files to this event
- Privacy
- Keywords

To demonstrate creating an event, we are going to create an event page for Human Resources Winter Party. At this point, we should be on the Create Event page. If not, we can click on the **Add Event** button to go to this page. We will use the following values for the fields on our form:

- **Title**: HR Winter Party
- **From Date**: January 13, 2011 02:00 PM
- **Body**: This year we will be sponsoring a local charity. Please bring a small unwrapped toy to be collected and donated
- **Notifications**: Click on **Notify all users**.
- **Keywords**: HR, Party, Winter Party, Directions

This event is going to be held off-site and we will want to attach a PDF file containing information about the event. Any PDF can be used to demonstrate attaching a document to the event. After filling in the preceding information, click on **Choose File** in the **Attach files to this event** section and select a PDF file to attach. The PDF will be uploaded to our site and should look similar to the following screenshot:

We can attach as many files as needed for our event. For example, we may want to attach an agenda, previous meeting minutes, and directions as three separate files.

Sometime the filename is not as friendly as we would like from the file we uploaded. We can change this by clicking on the **Rename** link next to the file. The new name will be saved with form when we click on **Save**.

The **List** checkbox allows us to specify whether this file should be available when users are viewing this event. By default, this is selected. There may be times when we want to attach a document for reference that is meant for administrators only. One example could be an attendee list. In this case, we will uncheck the **List** checkbox. The file will still be associated with this piece of content, but will not be displayed when a non-administrator is viewing the event.

The following screenshot is an image of the top half of our Create Event page after we have filled in all the values:

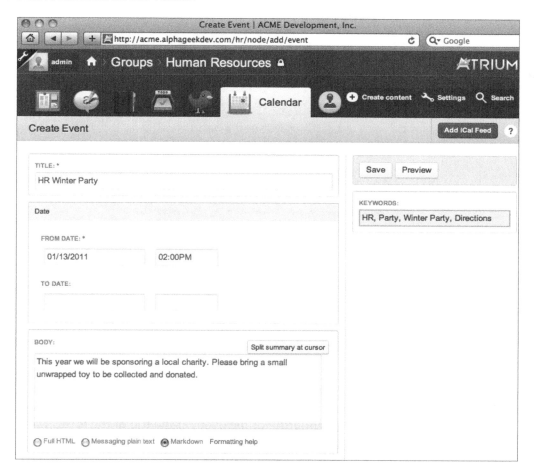

And the bottom half of the page is shown in the following screenshot:

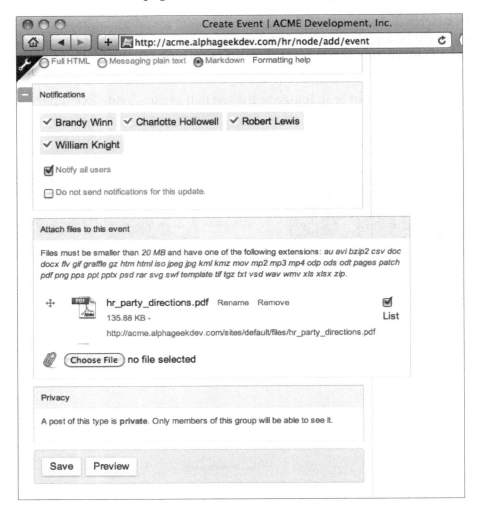

Once we have confirmed that we have filled in all the necessary fields for this event, we can click on **Preview** to see a rendering of the event at the top of the form. This is handy if we want to add some simple HTML to aid in formatting. We can make minor tweaks by previewing, editing the text, and then clicking on **Preview** again or **Save**. For this example, we will not be using any HTML and can go ahead and click on **Save** located at the bottom of the form or at the upper right corner.

You may notice that when you click on any date field, you get an easy-to-navigate mini-calendar that can be used to set the date. The following screenshot shows an example of the mini-calendar:

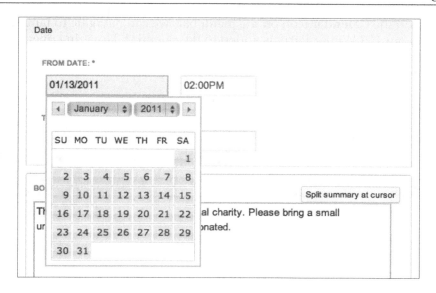

At this point, we have saved the event and a message will appear briefly at the top of the screen explaining that users were notified and the event was created. The message will disappear and we will be on the main View screen of the event. Our event view screen should look like the following screenshot:

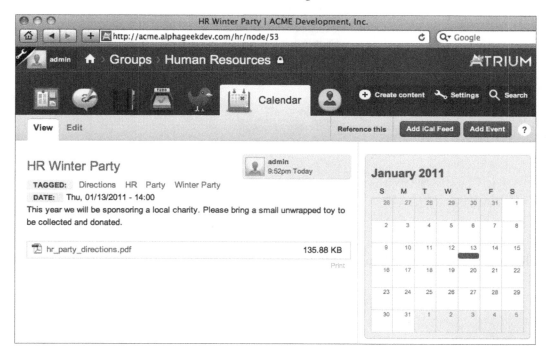

By clicking on the **Calendar** icon on the menu bar, we can navigate to January 2011 and see that our HR Winter Party is added to the calendar. Hovering over the event will provide a nice little tool tip with the date and title of our event as indicated in the following screenshot:

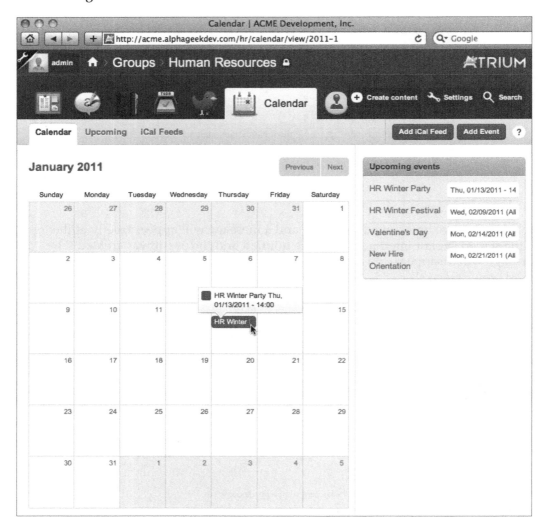

Clicking on the event will take us to the event View page.

Editing an event

After adding our event, we realized that we neglected to associate an end time with the event. This is important because the HR department only has the party space reserved until 6:00 PM. The Human Resources department also had to reschedule the event for January 6, 2011. These changes are easy to make through the Edit Event screen. We should be on the View screen for our HR Winter Party event that looks similar to the following screenshot:

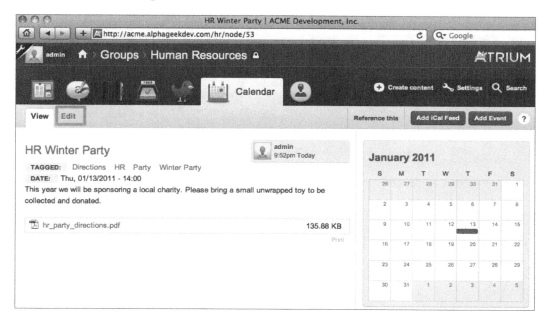

If not, we can locate the event on the main Calendar page and click on the event to return to this screen.

Once on the Edit screen, we notice that the **To Date** field has been filled in for us. This is because the **To Date** field is automatically filled in if it is blank when we save an event. We need to edit the event to change the date and provide an end time. By clicking on the **From Date**, we can select the new date, January 6, 2011 from the mini calendar. Next we will click on the date for the **To Date** field changing the date to January 6 as well and also changing the time to 6:00 PM. When completed, our edited event form should look like the following screenshot:

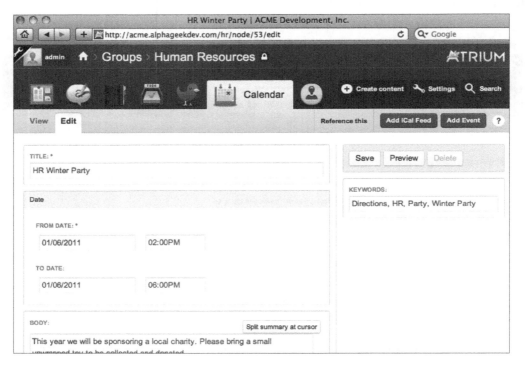

We can now click on the **Save** button on the top right to save our changes.

Now that we have edited the date and time for our HR Winter Party, we can click on the **Calendar** icon and navigate to January 2011. When we hover over the event, we will see that our tool tip has been updated to include the start and end time of the event. This should help avoid any confusion when the HR administrators begin asking people to leave at 5 or stay and help clean up. The following screenshot shows the updated version of our event when we hover over the event:

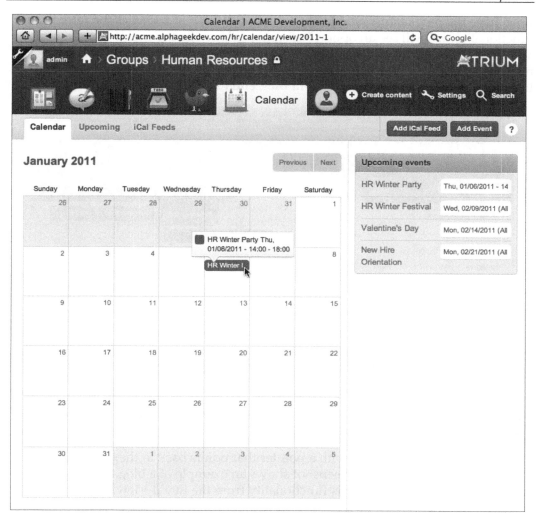

If we have the blog feature enabled or another feature that provides the referencing functionality, we will see an option **Reference this** on the top menu. This feature allows us to click on this link, choose a content type, and create a new page referencing the current event we are viewing. The following screenshot shows the location of **Reference this** and then **via Blog entry** options on the menu bar:

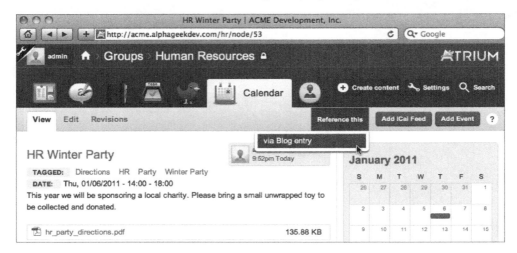

After clicking on the **via Blog entry** link, we will be on the Blog entry page.

 For more information about blog entries, you can refer to *Chapter 8, Blogs*.

The new page will be created with a pointer that points back to the event page for more details. The following screenshot shows an example of a blog entry that was created using the **Reference this** functionality from the Event View page:

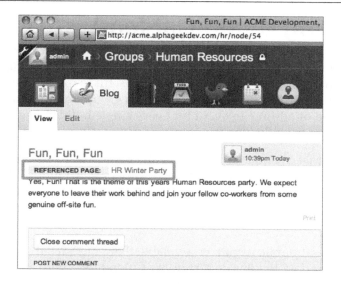

Clicking on the **REFERENCED PAGE** link under the blog title will take the viewer directly to the Event View page. A reciprocal link is provided at the bottom of the page that is referenced by other pages. In this case, a chart is appended to the bottom of our event View pages that provides a link to the referencing page, the time it was posted, and who the author was. The following screenshot shows an example of our event View page showing the blog entry that references this page:

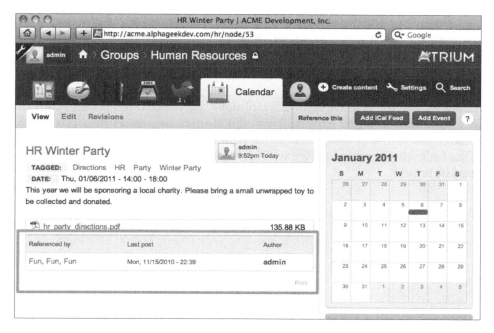

Subscribing to an iCal feed

In this section, we will show how to bring external data into our Open Atrium installation. After creating our first couple of Calendar entries, we might begin to think about other Calendar data that could be useful to display on our group's Calendar. One example, for the Human Resources group, might be a calendar of holidays. Instead of adding an event for every single holiday, we can pull in a calendar of holidays provided by an external source.

To bring in an external calendar source, we will need the iCal address for the calendar. Most external calendar feeds and applications (Apple's iCal, Outlook, Evite, Google) provide an iCal address. We may have to do a little digging or search the help text for our application to find the iCal feed. If we are using an application with multiple calendars, then the iCal address should be in the same place for each calendar.

There are also several public resources available that you can subscribe to and pull in external calendar data to your department's Calendars. There are many different types of calendars, ranging from phases of the moon to our favorite team's football schedule for the season. Our company may have a conference room calendar already set up in another application. If that application provides an external iCal feed, then we can pull that calendar's information into our system.

As the ACME Development Company is located in the United States, we are going to demonstrate how to add a US Holidays calendar. ACME already had a Google calendar for public US Holidays set up. To obtain the iCal link, we went on to our settings page for the US Holidays calendar and clicked on **iCal**. This created a window with the following URL for the iCal feed:

```
http://www.google.com/calendar/ical/en.usa%23holiday%40group.v.calend
ar.google.com/public/basic.ics
```

Now that we have the iCal Feed for US Holidays, we need to navigate to the Human Resources calendar in Open Atrium. From the Human Resources dashboard, click on the **Calendar** icon and then click on the **iCal Feeds** button on the menu bar at the top. In the following screenshot, we will highlight the **iCal Feeds** option and the **Add iCal Feed** buttons:

Adding an iCal feed form is probably one of the simplest forms we will encounter in Open Atrium. Each feed that we want to add has a **Title** and a **URL** field. The **Title** field will be for our reference when locating or reviewing the feed and the **URL** will be the iCal link that begins with `webcal://`. For Title we will use `US Holidays` and for URL we will use the link obtained from the iCalShare site. When both of these fields are completed, our form will look like the following screenshot:

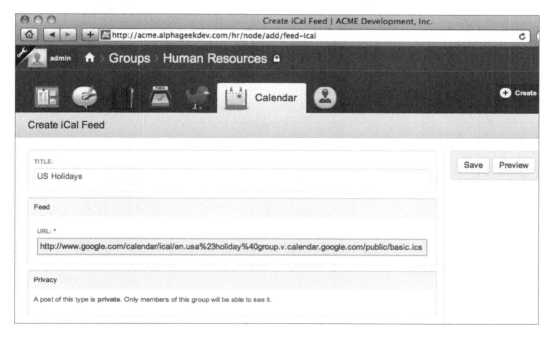

Clicking on **Save** will then import the Calendar items from the external source provided.

The Calendar feeds are maintained through a cron job that will run periodically to check and see if there are any feed updates. Running cron will be discussed in more detail in *Chapter 12, Open Atrium and Drupal Maintenance*. We can also navigate to the iCal feed at anytime and click on the **Import** link to bring in new items.

The following is an example of our January 2011 Calendar after adding and saving the iCal Feed for US Holidays:

We can see from the preceding screenshot that two holidays have been added to our January Calendar, **New Year's Day** and **Martin Luther King Day**.

Sometimes a Calendar feed may not import correctly into Open Atrium. In those cases, the problem is most likely to be caused by the feed itself and it is better to obtain a different source for the iCal feed you are trying to add.

There may be times when a feed gets stuck or we want to ensure that we have the most updated information and want to clear out any existing items in the feed. To do this, we can click on the feed title from the iCal Feeds screen and click on **Delete items**. This will delete all of the items within the feed and allow us to import the items again.

We may also want to delete a feed that is no longer used. To delete the whole iCal feed, including the items associated with it, click on the feed title from the iCal Feeds screen and click on **Edit**. Then on the right sidebar click on **Delete**. It will ask for confirmation that you want to delete this feed. After clicking on **Delete**, the feed and its items will be completely removed from our system.

Summary

One of the most important items of an Intranet is the concept of a shared Calendar. In this chapter, we learned how to use the Calendar feature of Open Atrium. In the first section, we walked through enabling the Calendar feature for individual groups and then reviewed the Calendar page.

In the next couple of sections we learned how to enter and edit Calendar entries, also referred to as events. Editing an event or Calendar entry is just like editing any other piece of content in the system with the exception of some added fields for tracking dates. We learned how to edit the date and time of an event using the **From date** and **To date** fields.

The last section of this chapter covered how to import iCal feeds from external sources into Open Atrium. This section walked us through the process of adding an external calendar source showing US Holidays to our group's Calendar page. The Calendar feature is not a complex feature, yet it has rich functionality, especially in its ability to pull in external data.

In the next chapter, we will go under the hood a bit more and look at how to customize our Open Atrium installation.

11
Customization

In this chapter, we will go under-the-hood of Open Atrium. Don't worry though, you should still be able to follow along and take what you learn to apply it to your company's Open Atrium installation. This chapter will cover the following topics:

- Case Tracker settings
- Site information

The first section, Case Tracker settings, will cover some basic changes that are easy to make to help us customize our Open Atrium installation to match better with our company's needs and terminology. We will cover how to modify some basic settings for the Case Tracker and how to modify views and assignee lists for Case Tracker fields.

The second section, Site information, will walk through the process of customizing the website name, and other small configuration settings that we can perform through the user interface of our installation.

Case Tracker settings

In *Chapter 9*, we walked through the process of setting up Case Tracker for your website to track issues and other items. We noted that the terminology may differ between companies and that some of the items such as priority and status can be customized to fit our company's terminology. In this section, we will walk through the process of customizing these settings.

The first thing we will need do is to ensure that we are logged in as the admin user, which is the first user that we created when we set up our site. When we are logged in as the admin user, we will see a wrench icon in the upper left corner of the screen. The following screenshot shows an example of the wrench icon, which is our gateway to the admin menu:

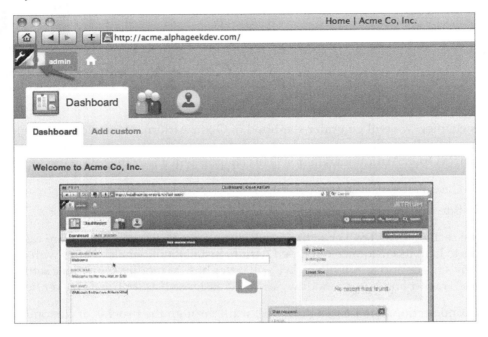

Clicking on this icon will reveal the administration menus for our Open Atrium installation. Once we click on the wrench, we can then click on the **x** on the top left corner of the menu to hide the administration menu, and click on the wrench again to show the menu. The wrench icon provides a convenient way to access the administration menu when logged in as the admin user. To begin customizing our Case Tracker settings, we will expand the administration menu and click on the **Site Configuration** link and then click on the **Case Tracker** link. After clicking on the **Case Tracker** link, our screen will look similar to the following screenshot:

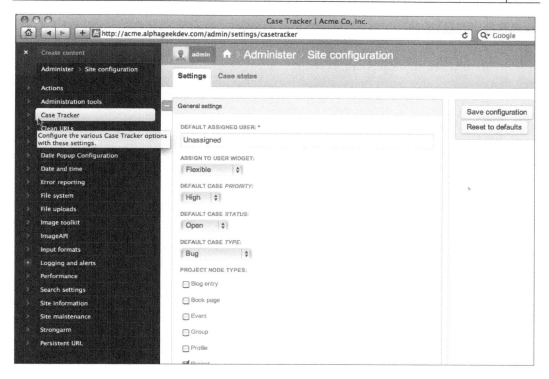

While configuring the Case Tracker settings, we can click on the **x** on the admin menu to hide it and move it out of the way. The first screen displayed is the Settings page, which allows us to modify some of the more basic Case Tracker settings. We will come back to this screen and will move ahead to configuring Case states.

Case states

The **Case states** tab is next to the **Settings** tab on the menu bar. After clicking on this tab, we should see the following screen:

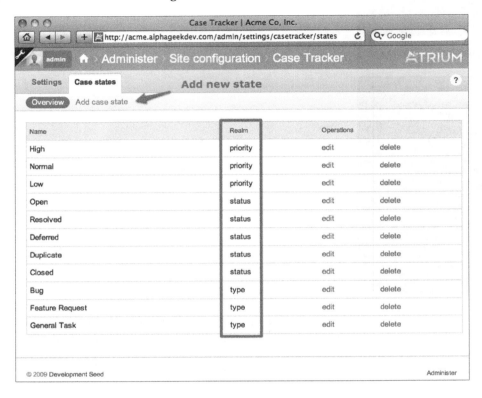

On this screen, we will see two links on the menu bar, **Overview** and **Add case state**. The first page displayed after clicking on **Case states** is the overview page. The Case Tracker module used with Open Atrium refers to the priority, status, and type items as realms. Each row on this page represents one of the drop-down values available for a specific realm. From this screen, we can choose to edit or delete any of these options by clicking on the links in the **Operations** column. To demonstrate the flexibility of the Case Tracker, we will modify priority to have two additional items, and change the names of some of the priority items.

Example 1: Modifying priorities

Acme Co, Inc. uses the following priorities instead of the default priorities that come with Open Atrium:

- Highest
- High
- Medium
- Low
- Lowest

With our initial installation of Open Atrium, we already have a high and low priority, and need our list to reflect three new priorities: highest, medium, and lowest. As we are not going to be using the normal priority, we can rename it to medium. By clicking on **Edit** on the row for the normal priority, we can access the edit page where we can change the name. The edit page will contain the following items:

- State name
- State realm
- Weight

The State name is the field that we want to change. We can erase the existing text, **Normal**, and type in our new label **Medium**. The State realm that we mentioned earlier determines which field group this value belongs to. In this case, we will leave it set to the priority realm. The weight field determines the sort order.

 Weight terminology is common across many different systems and is used to determine the sorting order of a set of fields. Lower weights will float to the top while higher weights will sink to the bottom of the list.

The weight field is useful for priorities because it will ensure that our priorities are in order from the most urgent to the least urgent. Once we have edited the **State Name** field, our edit page should look like the following screenshot:

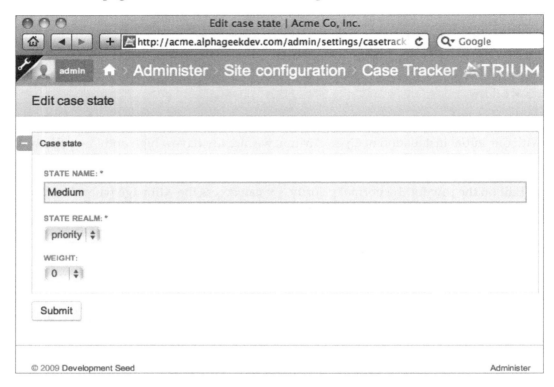

Now, we can click on **Submit** to save our changes, and on the Overview page, we can see that **Normal** has been replaced with **Medium**.

We still need to add the highest and lowest priorities. Clicking on **Add case state** on the menu bar allows us to add a new priority, type, or status. We can go ahead and click on **Add case state** to add our two additional priorities. For **STATE NAME**, we will enter **Highest** and confirm that the **STATE REALM** is set to **priority**. For the **WEIGHT** field, we will want to use a lower number, so that this item floats to the top of the priority list. In this example, we will set the weight to **-10**, so that the **Highest** priority floats to the top of the list. The following screenshot shows how the **Add case state** screen should look like before clicking on **submit**:

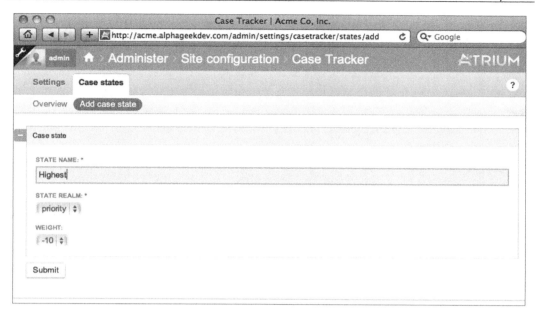

After clicking **Submit**, we can repeat the preceding steps to add the lowest priority option. For this priority, we will change the **Weight** to a higher number, so that it sinks to the bottom of the priority list. The lowest add form will look like the following screenshot:

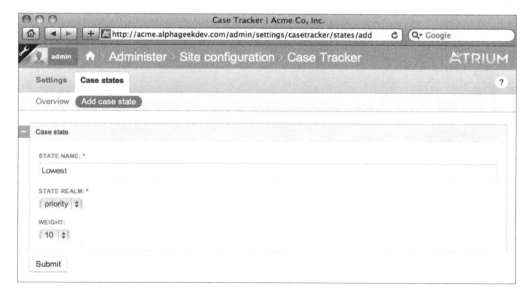

Again, we will click on **Submit** to change our settings and add our new priority. Now, we should have all of statuses renamed the way we want them to be and in the correct order. The Overview list should like the following screenshot:

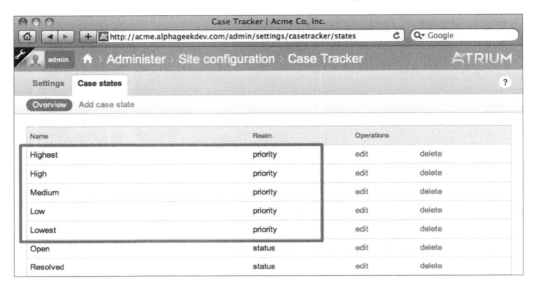

To see these changes in action, we will look at the Case Entry screen. Click on the home icon on the upper menu next to our login name, to return to our site's home page. The following screenshot shows the location of the home icon:

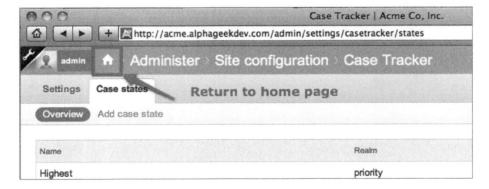

From the home page, we can then click on the **Human Resources** or **Information Technology** links at the right-hand sidebar to go to our group, as indicated in the following screenshot:

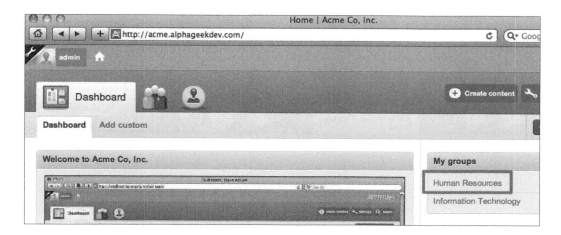

For this example, we will click on the **Human Resources** link and then click on the **Case Tracker** icon on the upper menu bar, as indicated in the following screenshot:

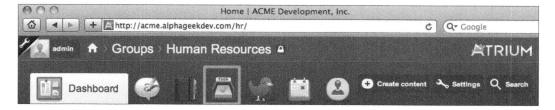

We now click on the **Add Case** button at the upper right side. This will take us to the Create Case screen where we can view the priority drop-down contained in the Case information section. By clicking on the drop-down, we can see our new priorities getting displayed in the correct order. The following screenshot shows an example of a newly modified priority list:

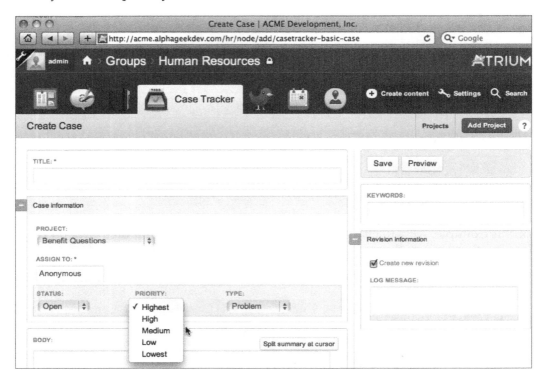

Any Case Tracker customization made through the admin interface (such as adding priorities, as shown in the preceding example) will be applied globally to all of our group pages. Unfortunately, at this point, we cannot make these changes based on an individual group's or department's page easily, as these changes are global. Most companies will probably use the same terminology throughout the company for the priority, status, and type. In the following example, we will walk through the process of modifying the **Case types** field.

Example 2: Modifying Case types

Acme Co, Inc. uses the following terms to describe their cases instead of the initial list that comes with our basic installation of Open Atrium:

- Inquiry
- New Feature
- Feedback
- Problem

As we are not going to be using any of the existing types, we can rename those and then add an additional type. The existing types will be renamed with the following new types:

Old type	New
Inquiry	New
New Feature	Feature Request
Feedback	General Task
Problem	Bug

First, we need to return to the Case Tracker configuration screen by clicking on the wrench icon to reveal the admin menu. Then we need to click on **Site Configuration | Case Tracker** to return to the Case states Overview page.

Now, we will rename **Feature Request** to **New Feature** and then repeat these steps for remaining case types. Clicking on the **Edit** link next to **Feature Request** will take us to the Edit screen where we can change the Case type name. This process is the same as the one that we followed to edit Case priorities.

Replace the text in the **STATE NAME** field with **New Feature**. We will leave **STATE REALM** and **WEIGHT** set to their existing values. Once we have edited the **STATE NAME** field, our edit form should look like the following screenshot:

Now, we can click on **Submit** to save our changes, and we will return to the Case states Overview page with the list of items. We can repeat the preceding steps for the remaining Case types to be renamed. After all of the Case types are renamed, the Case states Overview page should look like the following screenshot:

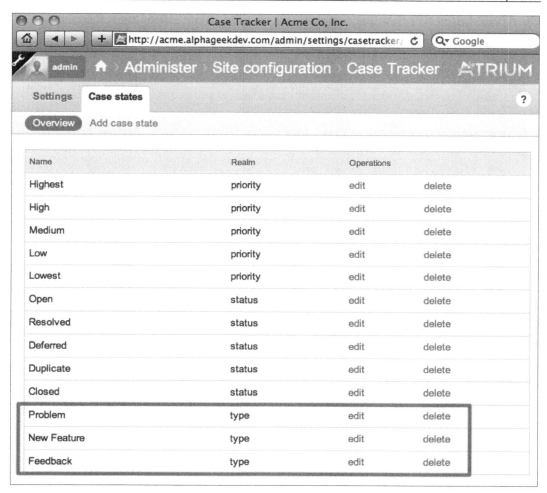

Now, the only thing left to do with types is to add an additional **Case type** for **Inquiry**. To do this, we can click on the **Add case state** link next to the **Overview** link, the same link that is used to add new priorities. For the **STATE NAME** field, fill in **Inquiry** and leave the existing values for **STATE REALM**, and **WEIGHT**. Then click on **Submit** to save our changes. Our new type will be added and will now appear in the Case type drop-down list for new and existing cases.

Our Case states Overview page should look similar to the following screenshot:

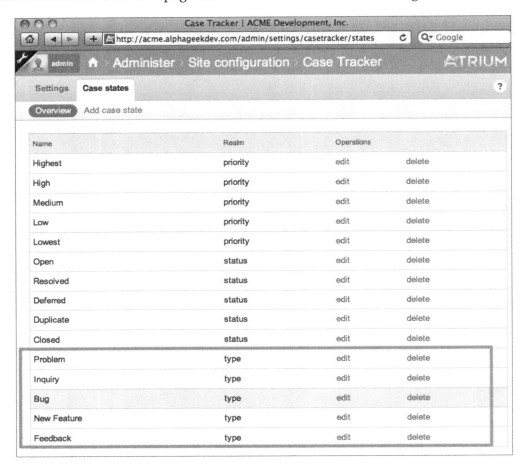

After modifying the Case types, we should have a solid understanding of how to make similar changes. The same methodology can be applied to other items, including the **Case status** field.

Settings

The **Case Tracker | Settings** page allows us to set defaults, assign the content types that render as projects or cases, and select custom views. The **Case Tracker | Settings** page is the first page displayed after clicking on **Site Configuration | Case Tracker** from the admin menu. The following image shows the top half of the **Case Tracker | Settings** page:

The following image shows the bottom half of the **Case Tracker | Settings** screen:

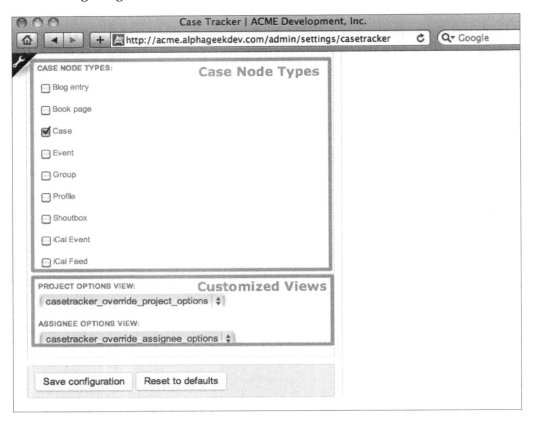

Defaults

The first section of the Settings screen contains the default values for our Case Tracker form. The default settings options allow us to set preselected items to be filled in when we first load the **Case Tracker** form. The following screenshot shows an example of the default settings screen:

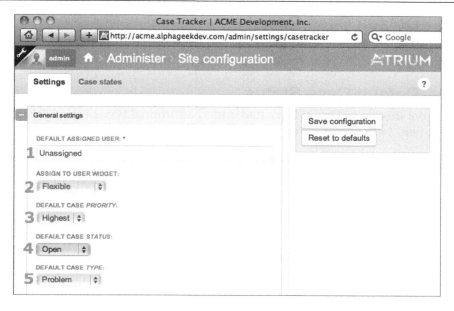

Item 1—Default Assigned User

In this section the **DEFAULT ASSIGNED USER** is set to **Unassigned**. Any new tickets that are created through the Case Tracker will not have a preselected assignee. We may want to change this, so that new tickets are automatically assigned to an assistant or administrator to filter through and reassign the tickets. To modify this option, we can click in the field and begin typing the username of the person we want to use for the default assignee. This form field is setup as an Autocomplete field and as soon as a match is found based on our typing, we can select that user.

Item 2— Assign To user Widget

This field allows us to set the format of how the assignee options are displayed in the Assign to field. The different options are:

- Flexible: Automatically determines how to present the **Assign to** user list based on the number of users.

- Select: Displays the users in a select list, and is useful if we have a large number of users in a group or department.

- Radios: Provides a radio button interface for users, and works well for a small number of users.

- Autocomplete: Allows the person entering the ticket to start typing a username and select a user.

Item 3—Default Case Priority

This field sets the default priority to be selected when entering a new case. If we do not want our default priority to be set to **Highest**, then we should change the value here.

Item 4—Default Case Status

We will leave this set to **Open**. If we had added additional types we might have had a different field to to preselect for the Default Case Status.

Item 5—Default Case Type

For this option, we will change the default value to **Inquiry**, so that any new tickets are not automatically assigned as a **Problem** case type.

Node types

Node types are divided into the following two sections:

- Project node types: The project node type allows us to customize our installation to have additional content types that are structurally set up to act as projects. Most sites will never need to add a new project type. Occasionally, there may be a time where we need to add a new content type and will need to configure it in this section to be recognized by Case Tracker as a project type.
- Case node types: Case node types is similar to Project Node Types in that it is not needed for a majority of the sites.

Customized views

The last section of the **Case Tracker | Settings** page provides options to select both the Project Options View and Assignee Options View. These two views provide the list of projects that are available for entering cases and the list of users that issues can be assigned to. For most sites we can probably leave these fields set to their default. There are some cases which we will discuss in the next section where we may want to change these.

Enabling views

To demonstrate the customized views' flexibility for Case Tracker, we must ensure that the **Views UI** module is enabled through the administration menu. To do this, we need to reveal the administration menu again and navigate to **Site Building | Modules**. A list of all the modules available for our site will be displayed on the screen. We need to locate the Views UI module and click on the checkbox next to it. Then we need to scroll down to the bottom of the screen and click on **Save Configuration**. The following screenshot shows an example of where the Views UI module is located with the checkbox already checked:

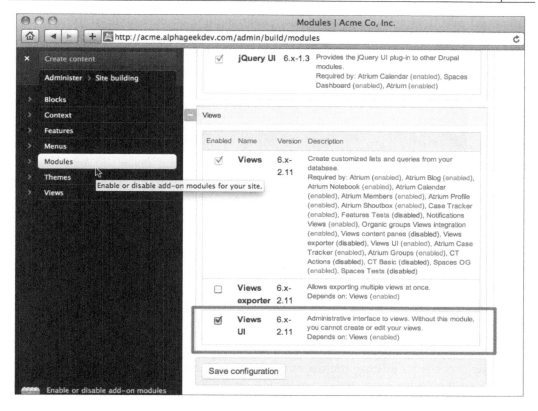

After enabling the module, you will see a new menu item under **Administer | Site Building** named **Views**. Navigate to and click on the **Views** link. A list of all the views for our site will be displayed. If you are more adventurous and curious, you may want to edit the different views and review their settings. From any view's configuration page you can click on **Cancel** at any time to revert any changes.

> The Views UI is considered a flexible query builder that allows users to create custom queries without having to know how to write SQL code (the code that interacts with the database) to retrieve data.

Assignee options view

This view allows us to filter or modify the list of users that are available to be assigned to a ticket. In most cases, this view will never need to be modified. However, we may run across a case where we need to limit the list of assignees for the cases and will want to modify this view. The next few paragraphs will walk through how to modify this view.

Prior to editing the view, we need to add a role that will be used to identify users that can be assigned cases. Open the admin menu and navigate to **Administer | User Management | Roles**. In the blank form field at the bottom of the screen, we can type **case assignee** and click on **Add Role**. The following screenshot shows an example of the **User Management | Roles** page:

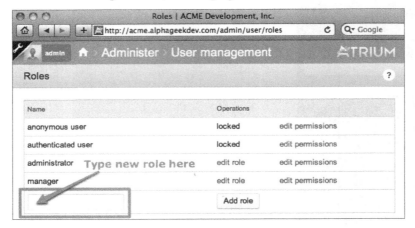

We also need to add the members who are responsible for adding cases to the case assignee role. To do this, we can refer back to *Chapter 4, User Administration* and follow the process for editing the user's or member's account settings. At the bottom of the account settings form, we can assign the member to the case assignee role.

Now, we are ready to modify the view. We will go the views admin page by navigating to **Administer | Site Building | Views | List**. Then we will locate the view titled **casetracker_override_assignee_options**, and click on **Clone**. It is about mid-way down the page and looks like the following:

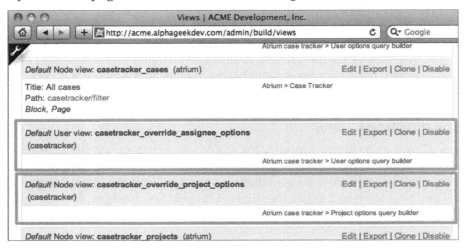

This will allow us to create a copy of the view to work with. For the **View Name**, we will want to change the name, so that our names do not conflict with existing views. For this example, we will name our view **casetracker_assignee_small**. We will leave all of the fields set to their defaults. The following screenshot shows the initial view screen after we have clicked on **Clone** and just before clicking on **Next**:

Clicking on **Next** takes us to the **Edit** page, which can be a little daunting at first. I encourage you to explore different options and read more about views, as they can be very powerful in extracting data.

The following image shows the view configuration screen for our cloned view:

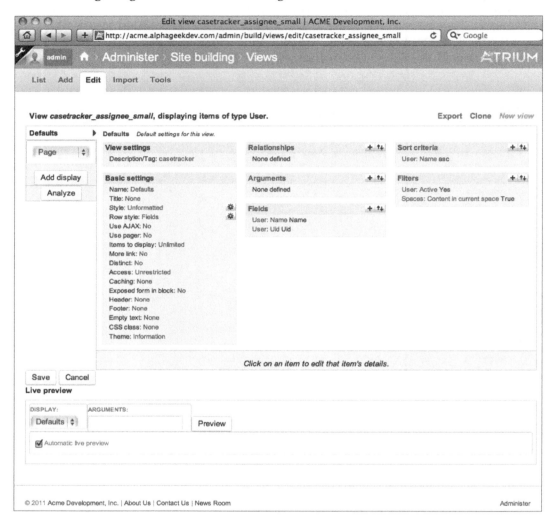

Now we need to locate the **Filters** section over on the far right and click the plus (+) sign to add a new filter. The bottom half of the screen will reload and then we can select **User** in the **Groups** select box. We then locate and check the box next to **User: Roles** and click on **Add**. The following is a screenshot of what the page should look like just before clicking on the **Add** button:

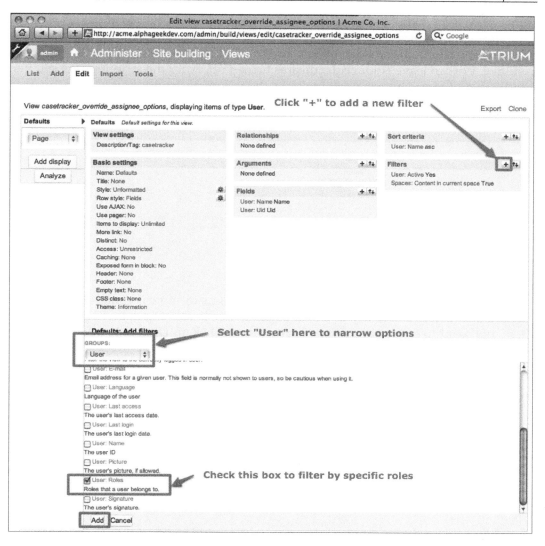

After clicking on **Add**, the middle part of the page will refresh to load the configuration options for **User Role**. For this example, we will want to keep the operator at the default of **Is one of** and under **OPTIONS** we will want to select **case assignee**. We can leave **Reduce duplicates** turned off. After these options are set, the middle part of our view page will look like the following screenshot:

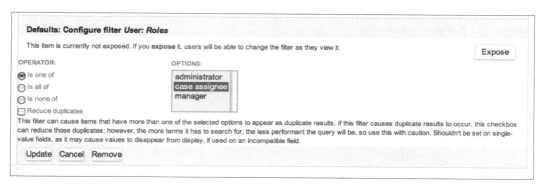

The **Expose** button in the upper right corner allows us to show certain filters to the user to allow him/her modify these filters as he/she is viewing data. For this view, we do not want to expose any filters. Now, we can click on **Update** to add the filter to our view. The final view screen will look like the following:

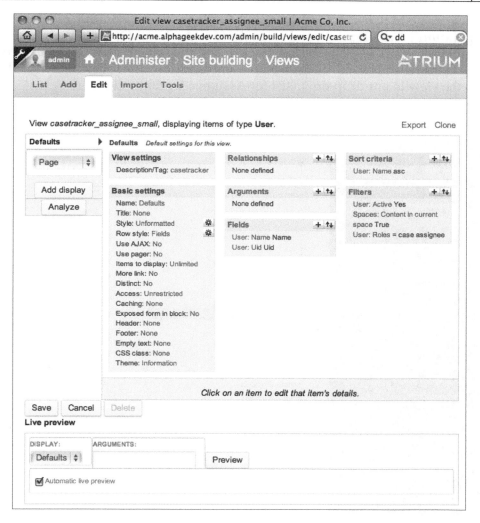

Now, click on **Save** at the bottom to save our changes to add our new view.

 Note, clicking on **Add** does not save the view. The view is not actually saved until the Save button is clicked.

Now we can go back to our **Case Tracker | Settings** screen (**Administer | Site configuration | Case Tracker**) and scroll down to **Assignee Options View** and we should see our new view, the **casetracker_assignee_small** view, in the list. We can select the new view and click on **Save Configuration**. The following screenshot shows the view in our drop-down list for **Assignee Options View**:

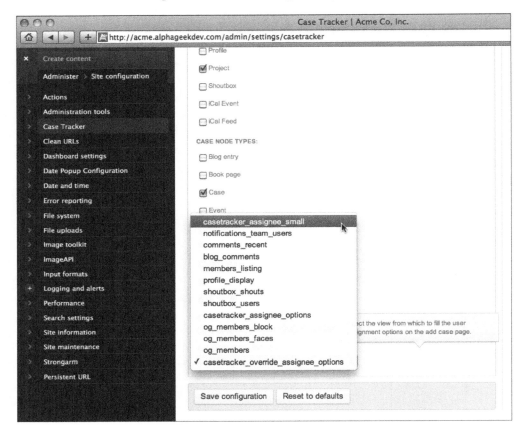

Now, when users enter new cases, only members or users who are assigned to the **case assignee** role will be available for the **Assign to** field. It does seem a little complex to complete such a simple task. Once you have edited a few views, you will start to see how powerful the Views UI really is.

Site information

Moving on from the **Case Tracker** we will look at customizing some basic Site Information settings. The Site Information page is the standard site information page that is used on any Drupal website. In *Chapter 12, Open Atrium and Drupal Maintenance*, we will cover more of the site maintenance and specific settings. This section primarily covers the basics, Site Name and Footer. We will edit the Site information form, just like any other page on our website. The following screenshot shows what the Site Information form currently looks like:

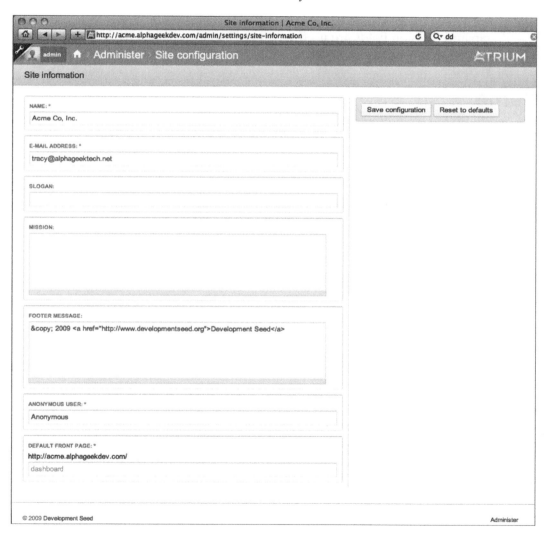

To get to the Site Information screen, we need to be logged in as an administrator and open the admin menu by clicking on the wrench icon. Then we can navigate to **Administer | Site Configuration | Site Information**. The Site information screen contains a number of fields, but we will be looking closer at the following four:

- Name
- E-Mail Address
- Footer Message
- Anonymous User

The Slogan and Mission fields are used on other Drupal websites with other Drupal themes to display snippets of text in particular places on the site.

Name

The first field that we will want to edit is the **Name** field. This is the site name that appears as the title on every page. The following screenshot shows where the site name is displayed on most browsers:

We can see from the preceding screenshot that the site name in the browser title bar matches the site name filled out on the form. Once we edit the site name and click on **Save**, then the browser title will also be updated. The text just before the site title, **Site information**, is actually the page title of the page we are on. The page title and site title together are used as the default name when a page from our site is bookmarked.

E-Mail Address

The next item is the e-mail address for the site administrator. This will be used as "the from address" when system e-mails are sent out.

Footer message

The next piece of information on this page that we are interested in is the Footer message. This is a flexible field that allows some HTML and can be used to set up a basic footer for our website without any programming. The default footer that shows up after installing Open Atrium looks like the one shown in the following screenshot:

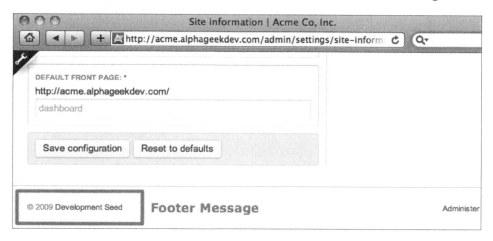

We can edit the footer message and add our own message to show up at the bottom of every page.

Anonymous user

The last piece of information that we may want to modify is the **ANONYMOUS USER** field. This field is used to label how we refer to non-logged in users. This field is more of a preference setting. Some companies like to label their non-authenticated users as 'visitors' instead of anonymous. This field is primarily used in administration screens. Although, we may see it crop up if you allow non-logged in users to post comments.

Editing the Site information form

We are going to change the values on the form to the following:

- **NAME:** ACME Development, Inc.
- **E-MAIL ADDRESS:** openatrium@acmeco.com
- **FOOTER MESSAGE:** © 2011 <a href="http://acme.alphageekdev.com" title="Acme Open Atrium site">Acme Development, Inc.</a> | <a href="about">About Us</a> | <a href="contact">Contact Us</a> | <a href="news">News Room</a>
- **ANONYMOUS USER:** Visitor

The following is what the form looks like just before we click on **Save configuration**:

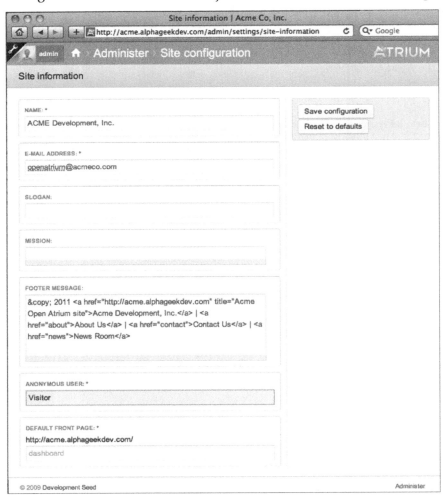

After clicking on **Save configuration**, we can log out and click on the home icon to return to the home page. If we have not created any public groups, the home page will redirect us to the login page. Click on the **Log in** button at the top left corner to go to the login page. We can see in the following screenshot that our settings from the Site information page are displayed:

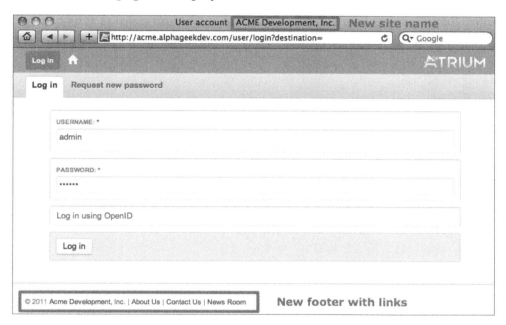

Summary

This chapter covered the following three main topics for our Open Atrium installation:

- Case Tracker settings
- Modifying views
- Site information

In the Case Tracker settings section, we walked through examples on how to edit basic settings for the Case Tracker, including default values, and how to modify the select lists for case status, priority, and type.

In the next section, we went through a brief introduction on how to edit views. We used the example of modifying the "Assign to list" in "Case Tracker" to only show users in the case assignee role. We looked at how to enable the Views UI module and learned how to clone a view to create our own working copy of the view.

Finally, the last section covered how to change the basic site information including the Site Name, E-mail Address, and Footer message. Thus, we were able to customize the browser title bar and footer message to match our companies terminology and branding.

In the next chapter, *Open Atrium and Drupal Maintenance*, we will dig a little deeper to find out what it takes to keep our Open Atrium installation running smoothly.

12
Open Atrium and Drupal Maintenance

In this chapter, we are going to move away from the front facing side of Open Atrium and focus more on the behind-the-scenes tasks to maintain our Open Atrium site. The good news is that Open Atrium is self-sufficient and requires little attention on a day-to-day basis. This chapter will cover the following two main topics:

- Routine maintenance
- Reporting

In the *Routine maintenance* section, we will cover tasks that need to be run on a periodic basis or when there is a specific problem. This section will include items such as running cron and applying site updates from newly released code. Then in the *Reporting* section we will find out how to view basic reports and logs to insure that our site is running in tip-top shape. We will begin the discussion with *Routine maintenance*.

Routine maintenance

As discussed earlier, our Drupal and Open Atrium site will run smoothly with very little attention being paid to it. The areas where we are most likely to run into problems will be when we try to upgrade the site, or when we customize the site and additional Drupal modules that were not included in the initial installation of Open Atrium. Drupal has a module called Features, which allows users to develop modules and allows them to be easily added to other sites. The Features module provides a mechanism for additional modules to be packaged together to create any additional views and apply configuration settings. As Open Atrium grows, more and more Features will be developed. These Features can then be downloaded from a Feature server and installed on our site. If a specific feature is developed for Open Atrium then upgrading should not be a problem. However, if we add additional modules from Drupal.org not included with Open Atrium, we risk our next upgrade to Open Atrium not working. The best thing to do when using modules outside of Open Atrium is to uninstall them before upgrading and then reinstall them after the upgrade. As the framework of the Drupal platform is so flexible, there are times where some things just do not work well together. If there is a particular module that would be useful in Open Atrium, I recommend engaging the Open Atrium community to work to add the module to a future release. Of course, if you are just tinkering with Open Atrium on a non-production site then I would go ahead and take a risk and try installing different modules. Now, let us move on to some of the routine tasks that need to be completed to keep our site running.

Running cron and search indexing

These two items go hand-in-hand because the only time search indexing happens is when cron is running.

What is cron?

On a Windows system this may be referred to as a scheduler or scheduled task. In its simplest form it is a job scheduler that allows us to define certain activities to take place at specific times with periodic intervals throughout the day. In Drupal, there is a special PHP page called cron.php, which, on our Open Atrium site is located at http://acme.alphageekdev.com/cron.php. After the page is loaded, we only see a blank page with no output. That is actually the expected result because this page is designed to run at the system level and expects no output.

Any module in Drupal can implement a function called hook_cron(). This allows each module to add its own maintenance functions to be performed every time that cron is run. Some of the examples of cron jobs might include the following:

- Sending out a daily e-mail with statistics on new users
- Blocking any account that has not logged in for over three months
- Performing an export of a specific table to a CSV file for additional processing
- Sending an e-mail to anyone that has not logged in since they signed up

We can see from the list that the type of tasks range from sending out e-mails to creating data export files. There really is no limit to what we can do with `hook_cron()`. The only requirement is that the `hook_cron()` function will be called every time the Drupal `cron()` function is run. If we were writing a custom module and only wanted to run it once a day, we would need to provide some mechanism to check to see if the job has already been run for the day. Otherwise, the job would run every time `cron()` is run.

You will want to talk to your host provider or your system administrator to figure out the best way to run a cron job in your environment. If you are not running on a Windows system and you have command line access to your server you may be able to run `crontab -e`, which will bring up the interface for adding cron jobs. The good news is that we can run this manually any time from the browser, which will assist us in insuring that our search index is kept up-to-date.

> For more information on hook_cron see the following pages:
> http://api.drupal.org/api/function/hook_cron/7
> http://drupal.org/node/347981
> http://drupal.org/cron

Search indexing

The search index walks through all the content on our site and creates an index so that when a user types in a search word our site can return a results page showing all the places where that word appears. In Open Atrium, the search box is located on the top right of a group or department's page, or we can access it by going to /search from the root of our website. The following is an example of the search box:

At this point, we have not run cron.php on our site and none of the content entries have been indexed. For example, if we type in the word **holiday** no results are returned on the search results page. The first thing we need to do is tell our Drupal install that we want to re-index the site on the next cron run. To do that, we need to log in as an administrator and go to the admin menu by clicking on the wrench icon. Then navigate to **Administer | Site configuration | Search Settings**. The top part of the **Search Settings** page will look like the following screenshot:

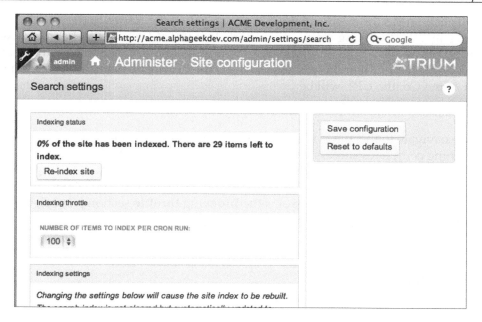

We can see that in the first section under **Indexing status** it states **0% of the site has been indexed. There are 29 items left to index.** Then it includes a button to **Re-index site**. This can be misleading at first because we might expect to find search results immediately after clicking **Re-index site**. However, all this does is to tell the module's cron hook that on the next cron run, we want to re-index the site. We will not see any search results until after the first cron run.

We will go ahead and click on **Re-index site** and then we should see the following confirmation box:

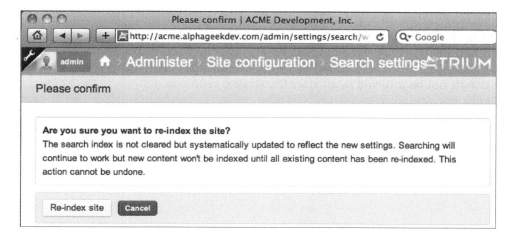

We will click on **Re-index site** again to confirm. When we return to the search settings page, the **Indexing status** still reports that **0% of the site has been indexed**. At this point, we have queued up the search module to re-index items on the next cron run. To run cron manually, we need to go the `cron.php` page of our site. In the case of Acme Co, the URL will be:

`http://acme.alphageekdev.com/cron.php`.

Once we navigate to this page, it may take a few minutes for cron to finish processing. If everything completes successfully, we will see a blank page. Now, if we return the **Search settings** page under **Administer | Site configuration | Search settings** we can see that the **Indexing status** says, **100% of the site has been indexed. There are 0 items left to index.** One item to take note of is the **Indexing throttle** section just below the **Indexing status** section, which we can see in the following screenshot:

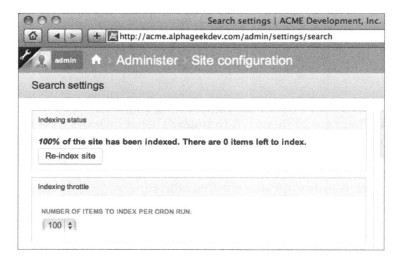

Indexing throttle tells cron how many pieces of content to process on each run. This means that the site may not be indexed 100% after each cron run. If we have 200 pieces of content and the **Number of items to index per cron run** is set to 100, then the site will not be indexed until after the second cron run.

Now, we can try our search again by returning to the home page and clicking on the search box and typing in **holiday**. We should see results similar to the list shown in the following screenshot:

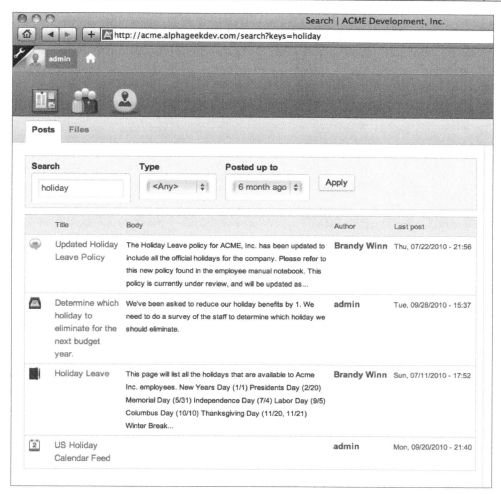

We can click on any of the links to view the contents of any of the items listed. Now, we know how to use cron.php and search settings together to maintain our search indexes. If users are not finding expected search results and we have added a considerable amount of content, this would be one of the first things to try. First we would queue the search page for re-indexing and then run cron several times until we had 0% of the items left to index.

An interesting note is that the **Search Results** screen is nothing more than a Drupal View. In *Chapter 11, Customization*, we learned how to modify the view for the **Assignee List** for the **Case Tracker** feature. The same methodology can be applied to the **search results** screen, which uses a view titled **search listings**. We could modify this view to not include the **Body** field so that the results will appear tighter on the page. The following screenshot shows the search results view without the **Body** field:

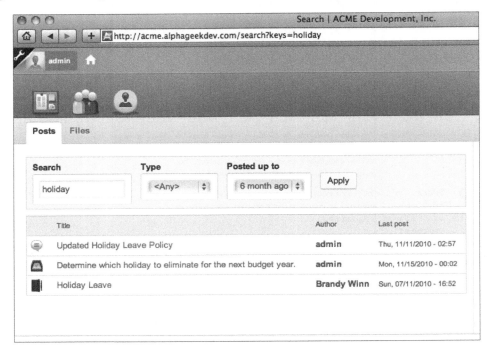

Rebuilding permissions

Another item that falls into the periodic or occasional maintenance category is rebuilding permissions. Rarely, will we need to do this, but every once in a while something will get hung up, and this will be one of the things we would want to eliminate as the cause. This usually creeps up as **Access denied** errors when accessing content that we know we have permission to see. Fortunately, this is an easy issue to resolve. We need to login as an administrator and go to the administration menu by clicking on the wrench icon. Then we can click on **Administer | Content management | Post settings**. The **Post settings** page will look like the following screenshot:

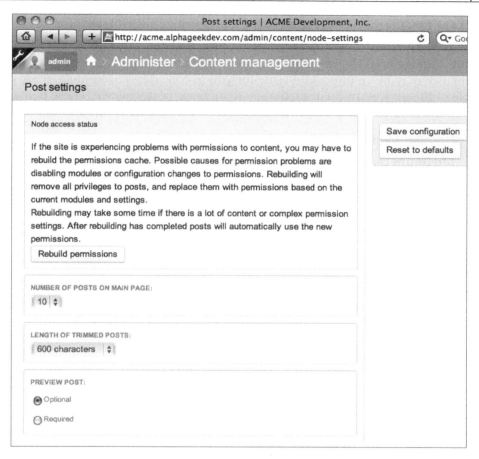

All we need to do is click the button labeled **Rebuild permissions** under the **Node access status** section. Then we need to click **Rebuild permissions** a second time on the confirmation page. The other settings can remain set as their defaults. The settings below the **Rebuild permissions** section allow us to tweak some of the following settings in a normal Drupal install.

- Number of posts on the main page
- Length of trimmed posts
- Whether creating/editing a new post requires a preview

Performance—caching

Drupal includes a basic caching system out of the box that most users will find sufficient for caching. Depending on the size of your Open Atrium install, performance may be an important issue for you to consider. Fortunately, there are a couple of things we can do immediately to increase performance. These items are found on the **Administer | Site configuration | Performance** page and include:

- Caching Mode
- Minimum cache lifetime
- Page compression
- Block cache
- Optimizing CSS and JavaScript files

Caching Mode

While logged in as administrator we can navigate to the **Performance** page (**Administer | Site configuration | Performance**). The first thing we will want to do is set **Caching Mode** to **Normal**. This will immediately improve performance for any anonymous user not currently logged in to your site. Drupal will store the cached pages and not have to regenerate the page with every request, thus increasing performance. We can also set a **Minimum Cache Lifetime** value that can be configured to only recreate the cache during specified intervals. This may be useful on higher traffic sites. New content will only appear when the cache is cleared manually, or when the **Minimum Cache Lifetime** has expired. The last item under caching mode is **Page Compression**. This only needs to be changed if your web server does not already perform page compression. The following is what the **Page cache** settings section looks like on the **Performance** page after changing the **Caching mode** to normal:

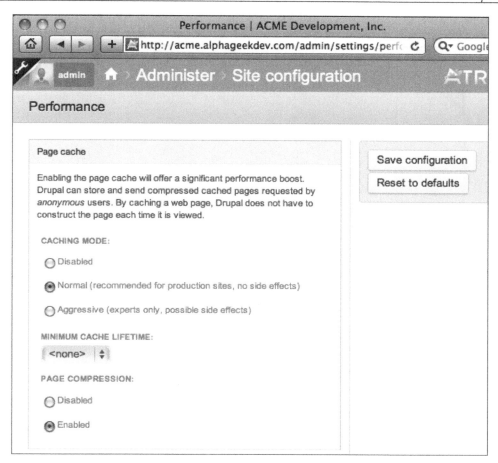

Block cache

This is a good performance tip to note for other Drupal sites. However, because Open Atrium uses modules which define their own content access restrictions, this option cannot be enabled on Open Atrium sites. Enabling the block cache will provide a small performance gain for authenticated or logged-in users. This prevents blocks from having to be reconstructed on every page load. If you already have caching turned on, then you may not see an increase for anonymous users, but should see a performance gain for authenticated users.

The following screenshot shows the **Block cache** section of the **Performance** page:

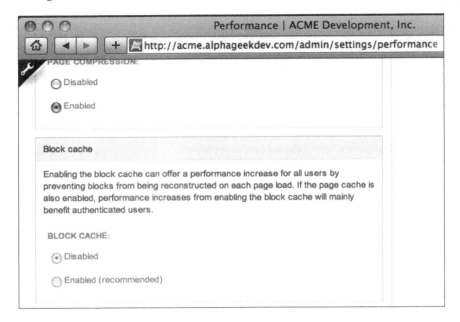

Bandwidth optimizations

The last section under **Performance** is **Bandwidth optimizations**. Drupal and many contributed modules include a large number of JavaScript and CSS requests. For each of these requests there is a call made from the browser to the web server to obtain these files. By enabling caching of these files, Drupal will read all the files required, remove white space from the file, and package the files up into one file each for JavaScript and CSS. This in turn will decrease page-loading time for our users.

One catch is that if we make any changes to the JavaScript or CSS, we may need to click on **Clear cache** (see the following section) or toggle the optimization from enabled to disabled and then back to enabled. This will force the compressed files to be regenerated. It is also worth noting that some browsers cache this compressed file as well and we may need to hold down the *Shift* key and click **Refresh** in our browser to force the outdated file to be removed.

After enabling the Optimization settings for CSS and JavaSript the **Bandwidth optimizations** will look like the following screenshot:

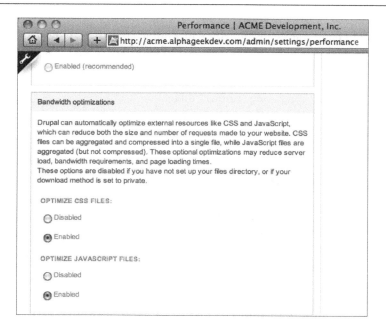

Clear cached data

This button is provided to manually force the cache to be cleared. It is useful when actively developing on the site or installing a new module. We can click this button at any time to force the site cache to be recreated. Sites with more traffic may see a brief slowdown while the data cache is rebuilt. The **Clear cached data** section looks like the following screenshot:

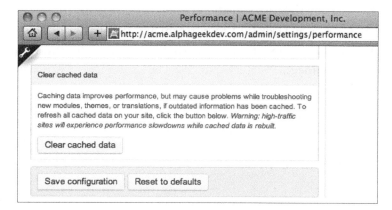

For small to medium sites these **Performance** settings may provide enough of a performance boost to prevent us from adding additional servers to handle site traffic.

If you have a large install, you will want to consult with industry specialists to determine the best techniques for scaling and performance tuning Drupal. For more information on scaling and performance tuning see the following links:

http://drupal.org/node/2601

http://loadstorm.com/2009/performance-tuning-drupal-10-good-links

Applying site updates

Upgrading our site needs to happen periodically for two reasons. The first reason is that released security updates should be applied to limit the vulnerability of our site. The second reason to upgrade is to take advantage of more stable releases and have access to new features that have been added to the site. Upgrading Drupal is fairly straightforward and it essentially requires you to:

1. Download the latest Drupal core code.
2. Backup your database and files including your sites directory.
3. Log in with User ID 1, the first account created.
4. Place the site in **Off-Line** mode (**Administer | Site Configuration | Site Maintenance**).
5. Move the /Sites directory temporarily.
6. Remove the existing files in the directory.
7. Uncompress the downloaded files.
8. Move the /Sites directory back.
9. Run update.php as User ID 1 to perform any database updates.
10. Place the site back in **On-Line** mode (**Administer | Site Configuration | Site Maintenance**).

An alternate way to upgrade your site is to use a program called Drush, which stands for Drupal shell. Drush is a listing or scripting utility that allow us to perform Drupal actions without having to go through the user interface. If you are comfortable with the command line, then you will probably want to take a closer look at Drush and upgrading via Drush.

For more information about Drush, visit:
`http://drupal.org/project/drush`
`http://drupal.org/node/477684`

Upgrading Open Atrium follows the same steps as the preceding bullet list. The only exception is that we will have to go to the Open Atrium website to download the new version. We can always find the latest Open Atrium version at:

`http://openatrium.com/download.`

Reporting

The title 'reporting' is somewhat misleading. It is the title Drupal uses to give to the page that allows us to view the following:

- Available updates
- Database logging
- Status report

Available updates

The first item we will look at is the **Available updates** page. This page provides a snapshot of the current version of modules that are available that have their code base stored in the Drupal CVS repository. Customer modules that do not have their code base stored in the Drupal CVS repository will not show up on this page.

As a general rule, we will not need to manually update any of the modules on our Open Atrium install even if a newer version is released. Instead, we should wait for the next full update of Open Atrium, which usually includes any newer stable released versions of the modules; although there may be an occasion or two where we need to upgrade a module outside of Open Atrium.

To access the **Available updates** page, we need to insure we are logged in as an administrator and navigate to the **Administer | Reports | Available Updates** page. The following screenshot shows the top portion of the **Available updates** page:

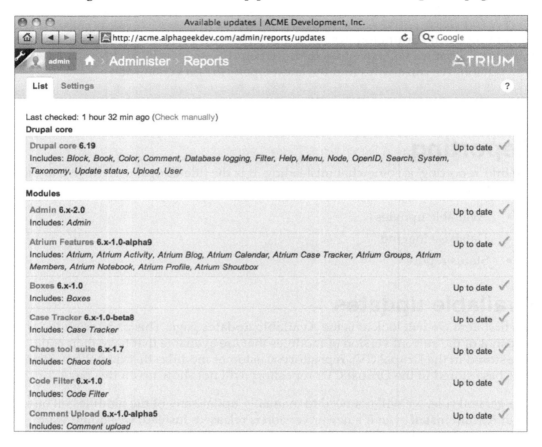

Modules with the green background and the words **Up to date** with a checkmark do not need updating. These modules are on the current stable released version of code. If a background is yellow then there is a newer released version. Red applies to any module that has a security update attached with it. Security updates should be applied as quickly as possible to avoid any potential vulnerability. However, depending on the severity of the update it usually is better to wait for a newer version of Open Atrium to be released that has been tested with the newer update. Usually new distributions such as Open Atrium are upgraded quickly after a security release. Distribution maintainer will try to incorporate the security update in as little as one to two weeks after a security update has been released.

Here is an example of the **Available Updates** page where one of the modules has a newer released version:

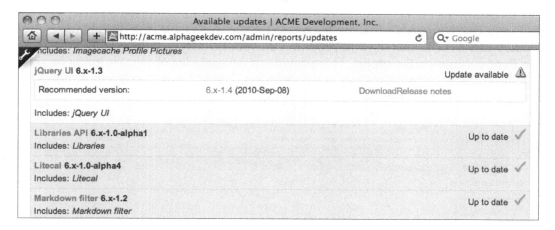

 For more information on upgrading modules visit the following URL: http://drupal.org/update/modules.

Database logs

There are four database log entries that we need to be aware of, for Drupal installations. These logs can assist us when troubleshooting problems and should be reviewed on a periodic basis. We can access these items from the same report menu by going to **Administer | Reports** while logged in as administrator. The four links on this page include:

- **Recent log entries**
- **Top 'access denied' errors**
- **Top 'page not found' errors**
- **Top search phrases**

The last three are self-explanatory and provide information about what is being searched and general errors with pages not found or where access was denied. This can be useful if we have migrated from a previous site and realize that there are some URLs that users are still using to locate content. We can use this log to determine which pages are still being accessed, and modify our web server configuration to redirect these pages to the correct place.

Recent log entries

This section will look at the **Recent log entries** report in more detail. By default our Open Atrium install has logging turned on. When we initially arrive on this page, we will see a list of messages that are logged to the database table called **Watchdog**. Any module can write to this log and provide a custom **Error type**, which shows up in the **Type** column on the report. This provides a general idea of what is going on with our site and where problems might be occurring. The following screenshot shows the first few entries of the **Recent log entries** page:

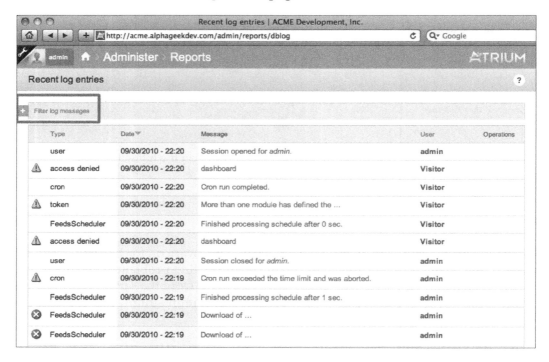

One item to note is that depending on our site traffic the watchdog table can grow rather quickly, with many pages of entries. To reduce the amount of data being filtered through, we can click the plus sign next to the **Filter log messages** at the top of the page to only show items in an area that we are concerned about. For example, if we want to see all messages related to **cron**, we could add **cron** from the list and click on **Filter**, as shown in the following screenshot:

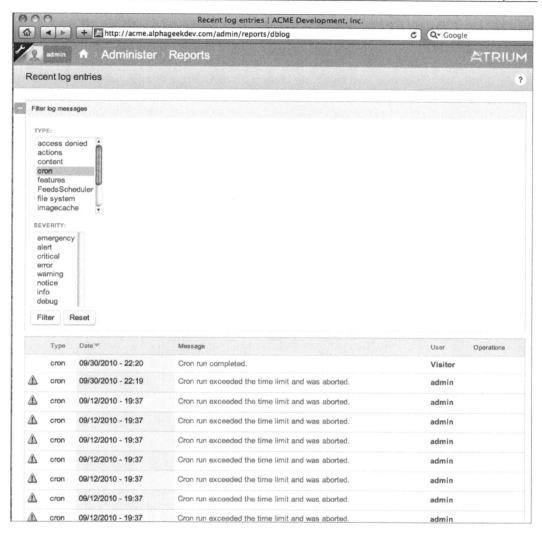

Now, only the cron-related messages are showing up in the list. We can also apply a filter to the message severity by selecting one or more of the severities in the **Filter** menu above.

When a site is running smoothly, it is easy to forget to review the Recent log entries report. However, we should continue to monitor this periodically. Also, the database logging module that produces these reports can be turned off at any time. If we have a high traffic site we may want to disable the module, as there may be additional overhead with database logging.

Status report

That last administrative piece we are going to cover is the Site status report. This report provides a brief summary of our site. It provides a quick health and sanity check. It tells us when was the last time cron was run, what version of Drupal we are running, and other useful information. If we have inherited a pre-existing site this is probably one of the first places we will want to go to review the basic configuration of our site. The status report can be accessed in the administrative menu by going to **Administer | Reports | Status Report**. The status report for our site looks like the following screenshot:

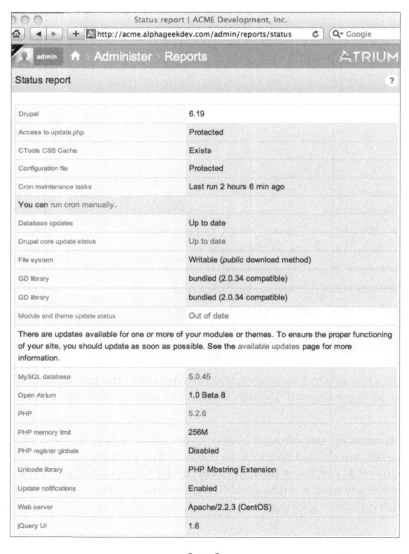

We can see that cron was last run 2 hours and 6 minutes ago, and that our PHP version is 5.2.6. This page also provides links back to the Available updates page for modules that have an updated version available.

Summary

This chapter walked through some of the routine basic maintenance tasks and looked at logging and reporting. In the first section of this chapter we looked at running `cron.php` and how to rebuild our search index. We learned that either our web server or another type of job scheduler should run `cron.php` periodically. Then we reviewed how and when to rebuild permissions.

The next part talked about caching and when we might want to use caching and Bandwidth Optimization for sites with a large number of users. We learned that block caching applies only to authenticated or logged in users, while general site caching only applies to non-authenticated users.

Next, we took a brief look at the recommended procedure for updating a Drupal site. We introduced a program called **Drush**, which provides shell to common Drupal tasks.

Finally, we looked at the Available updates, Status report, and Recent log entries pages. All of these items provide valuable data when we are determining how well our site is running, when something needs to be updated, and what types of errors might occur.

This chapter only touched on a few of the administrative tasks for Drupal. These topics should cover about 90% of what we will have to do in Drupal, and provide a good reference for troubleshooting a Drupal and Open Atrium site.

Resources

Drupal resources

As Drupal becomes more popular and with the release of Drupal 7, there are many resources available to learn more about Drupal or assist you with your own Drupal installation. This section will walk through various sections of the `Drupal.org` website and then provide a list of additional links at the bottom.

Drupal.org

There is a ton of information on the `http://drupal.org` website to sift through. This section will attempt to highlight some important parts.

Documentation

The `http://drupal.org/handbook` section contains several handbooks that can be used for increasing your Drupal knowledge or troubleshooting a problem.

If you are new to Drupal, then you will probably want to spend a lot of time in the "Getting Started with Drupal" section, which currently contains the following handbooks:

- Understanding Drupal
- Installation guide
- Administration guide
- Structure guide
- Site Building guide

The next section "Writing Your Own Code" is a great section for developers. It includes the following handbooks:

- Developing for Drupal
- API reference
- Examples for developers

This section contains the API reference that documents every Drupal function and is a must for any Drupal developer to look up syntax, or how a specific function works. The developing for Drupal handbook is also a great reference for Drupal development best practices. The remaining handbooks on this page include Tutorials, Reference, and Community.

As you read through the documentation, you may find gaps or parts that are not clear. One of the beauties of open source software is that anyone can contribute. This not only applies to programming but also applies to documentation.

The first thing that you will want to do, if you have not done so already, is sign up on `Drupal.org`. This will enable you to log in and communicate with other `Drupal.org` users through their personal contact form. You can follow the links on the documentation page to read more about contributing to the documentation effort.

Download

The `http://drupal.org/project` section of the website contains all of the contributed code from the community, as well as the Drupal core. This section includes the following:

- Drupal project—core files
- Installation profiles
- Modules
- Themes
- Theme engines
- Translations

Probably the most used section will be the modules section. Modules are packaged pieces of code that can be added to a Drupal website and enabled through the site administration to take advantage of their functionality. On the module section, you can search for modules by categories, by Drupal version, or by keyword. This section provides a good overall view of what Drupal can do and the power of open source contributed code.

Other sections

There is a wealth of information on the `Drupal.org` website. While browsing the website, you will find information on support, how to give back to the community, translations, consultants, and more.

General Drupal resources

This section contains a list of links with a short description describing each link. The following are links that I find handy as a developer:

Link	Description
`http://groups.drupal.org`	Place for groups by specific topic or location. Great place to interact with other Drupal developers. Sometimes referred by developers as the GDO (groups.drupal.org).
`http://planet.drupal.org`	This is an awesome site that aggregates feeds from the most active Drupal community members.
`http://lynda.com`	Not Drupal specific but contains several lessons on Drupal 6 and Drupal 7.
`http://drupal.org/irc/channels`	Internet Relay Chat — provides channel references to obtain live support and chat for various Drupal issues.
`http://acquia.com/downloads`	Provides a free distribution of Drupal with many common modules already pre-installed.
`http://association.drupal.org/`	Provides funding, infrastructure, and events to support the Drupal project.
`http://www.drupaldude.com/`	A site to help you learn Drupal and its modules.
`http://crackingdrupal.com/`	Provides excellent discussion on how to protect your site from security vulnerabilities as you build your code.
`http://drupal.org/hosting`	List of Drupal hosting companies.
`http://drupal.org/training-services`	Additional links for Drupal training.
`http://www.drupalmodules.com/`	Alternate search for Drupal modules.
`http://drupalsn.com/`	The Drupal social network.
`http://php.net`	The main website for PHP.net. Useful for looking up syntax.
`http://mysql.com`	The main website for MySQL.
`http://drupaldojo.net/`	Training for the Drupal community.
`http://drupalcodesearch.com`	Search page for Drupal code snippets.

Drupal distributions

Since this is a book about Open Atrium, it wouldn't be fair to not talk about Drupal distributions. Drupal distributions are pre-packaged versions of Drupal that are designed for a particular set of functions or tasks. They are also referred to as **Installation Profiles** on the Drupal.org site (http://drupal.org/project/installation+profiles). Open Atrium is a perfect example of a Drupal distribution that packages the existing core functionality, adds configuration, and additional modules.

Open Atrium

http://openatrium.com is the first and foremost website for information about Open Atrium. This website has some useful information on features and contributing, as well as links to documentation, the latest code, and system requirements.

The following are the important links for Open Atrium:

Link	Description
http://openatrium.com/documentation/requirements	System requirements
http://openatrium.com/features	Explains some of the features
http://openatrium.com/contribute	How to contribute
http://openatrium.com/download	Links to previous and latest
https://community.openatrium.com/	Documentation, issue tracker, and business resources
http://community.featureservers.org/fserver	Feature server
https://community.openatrium.com/documentation-en/node/441	List of contributed features

Calendar feeds

The last section of resources provided is a couple of links to some useful Calendar feeds. Many applications whether public or private provide iCal feeds. Check with your particular application to see how to export a Calendar as an iCal feed. Usually, you can just do a Google search for iCal and the name of your application.

Here are a couple of calendar feed lists:

Link	Description
http://icalshare.com	Holidays, sports, religious
http://icalworld.com/	Holiday, restaurants, political, sports
http://www.apple.com/downloads/macosx/calendars/	Week numbers, moon phases, sports,
http://www.calendarlabs.com/ical-calendar-holidays.php	Holidays only

B
Features & Theming

One of the most beautiful things about Drupal is its extensibility. As a result of the way the Drupal platform is architected, you can easily build features to use on your own websites. As all of the modules should follow the same set of rules, most features will work together and not have any conflicts. Occasionally, we may run into a module that is written poorly and may cause problems. In developing Open Atrium, the developers also created a module named **Features**.

What is a Feature?

In Drupal, the code from a module may need configuration changes through the user admin interface. If we developed a module to distribute to our regional offices, we would need to provide instructions on how to create a view, make configuration changes, and install the module. The Feature module packages these changes into a module that can then be installed and updated on other servers.

The Blog and the Calendar features in Open Atrium are an example of modules implemented using the Features module. When these features are enabled on a particular website, they check to ensure that all dependencies are enabled before installing the features. One benefit of Features is that you can modify a portion of a feature through the UI and any point in time revert back to the original version on the `/admin/build/features` page. This also helps in keeping your website updated. As new code for a particular feature is released, sites can be automatically updated.

The Features module provides a mechanism to store custom module configuration settings in the code base. For example, suppose we had a custom module that created a new content type and a view. Before the view can be created, the content type would have to be created. The Features module allows us to store these actions in a module, so that when the custom feature is enabled, the content type will be created along with the view. This provides the flexibility to revert back to the original version.

Contributed features

One of the goals of the Features module is to provide users with the ability to share features easily. While `Drupal.org` is a great place to share community-contributed modules, the creators of Features think that there is a better solution for sharing features. The idea is to create a network of Features servers that include the ability for users to download specific features. For example, if a view for a specific layout for a Blog page is created, then other community members should be able to download and install that same view rather than trying to create a view on their own.

In this section, we will review an example of how to add an already developed Feature to our website. This will be important, as more and more developers create Features for Open Atrium. We can locate these features on a Feature server and then download and use them on our website without any additional coding. We will also look at references to supplemental documentation on how to create our own feature.

Locating the community contributed features

As the Features functionality continues to be developed, additional Feature servers will become available. The following link provides a list from `groups.drupal.org` with a set of current feature servers:

`http://groups.drupal.org/node/50278`

Writing your own Feature

Of course, we do not have to wait for someone to release a specific Feature; we can create our own Feature. It is not that different from creating our own module. We just need to to ensure that everything is exportable and written back to our module files.

To begin, we will need to install the Features module and any dependencies. Once that is complete, we can write our module normally. Then we can go to the create page for the features module located at `/admin/build/features/create` and fill out the necessary information on a page that looks like the following screenshot:

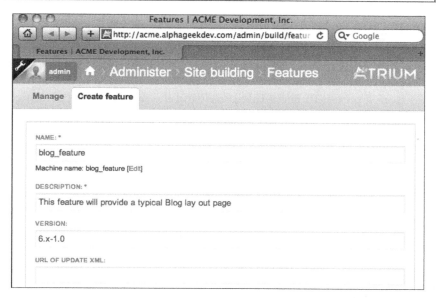

Once we have exported our Feature, we will have a set of files that can be edited which we will add to our module. Then we can package it up and install it on any server with features enabled by going through the site administrator and enabling the new feature.

There are a few more steps other than what is listed above. For the most part, these are the basic steps that we would go through to write a Feature.

The Features functionality makes Open Atrium a great product by allowing other developers to easily make pluggable functionality that can be added to a websites code base. It allows Open Atrium to be extended by the community which in turn allows us to consume those features on our website. This Appendix does not give the Features functionality the amount of coverage that it deserves.

For more information about Features visit the following URLs:

- `https://community.openatrium.com/documentation-en/node/1943`
- `http://openatrium.com/build_a_feature`
- `http://developmentseed.org/blog/2009/sep/03/5-minute-feature-server`
- `http://developmentseed.org/blog/2009/jun/26/recipe-feature-server`
- `http://developmentseed.org/blog/2009/jun/24/distributed-feature-servers-drupal`
- `http://developmentseed.org/blog/2009/may/29/making-and-using-features-drupal`

Theming

In this book, we touched on some areas where we can add our own colors or logos, but what if you wanted to give the Open Atrium website a whole makeover? We can do that with a custom subtheme. A subtheme allows us to take advantage of theming information from a parent theme while providing the flexibility to customize various parts of the themes. By using a subtheme, we do not need to reinvent the wheel and create a whole theme from scratch. The Open Atrium community website provides detailed instructions on how to create a subtheme for Open Atrium located at the following URL:

`https://community.openatrium.com/documentation-en/node/1961`

The basic process for creating a subtheme in Open Atrium is as follows:

1. Create a Ginkgo subtheme.
2. Design custom image overrides.
3. Setup our subthemes directory.
4. Add custom sprites and any other images.
5. Add custom CSS.

The images are fairly easy to customize and we can use sprites to edit a majority of the images at one time. If you are already familiar with Theming in Drupal, then this process should come fairly natural to you. If you are not familiar with Drupal Theming, then you can follow the link given in the preceding paragraph and learn more about custom theming and creating subthemes. For more information refer to the subtheme documentation from the link listed above and scroll down to the bottom of the page.

Index

D

dashboard
  about 85
  Create content button 93
  group dashboard 88-90
  main dashboard 86, 87
  modifying 93, 94
  Private Group 94
  Public Group 94
dashboard, modifying
  about 93
  block items 97
  block items, calendar 98, 99
  block items, message of the day 99, 100
  Create content button 93
  Description field 95
  layout, changing 96
  Path field 95
  Private Group 94
  private group, creating 94
  Public Group 94
  Title field 95
dashboard section, user admin tasks 80
database
  creating 42, 44
  creating, on Mac (MAMP) 42, 43
  creating, on Windows (WAMP) 43
  Mac (MAMP) & Windows (WAMP) 44
  user, creating 44-46
database logs, reporting
  recent log entries 264, 265
Default Assigned User field, case states 231
Default Case Priority field, case states 232
Default Case Status field, case states 232
Default Case Type field, case states 232
directory view 118
document library. *See also* notebook
document library, Open Atrium 15
Drupal
  about 7
  content management system, functions 8
  downloading, ways 46
Drupal administration, Open Atrium
  about 56
  administration menu 60
  administration section 58, 59
  Open Atrium, home page 57

Drupal.org
  documentation section 269, 270
  download section 270
  other sections 271
Drupal resources
  about 269
  Drupal distributions 272
  Drupal.org 269
  general Drupal resources 271
  URL 271
Drush
  URL 46

E

e-mail field, site information 243
event, calendar
  creating 199-204
  editing 205-209

F

features module
  about 275
  community contributed features,
    locating 276
  contributed features 276
  feature, writing 276, 277
  URL 277
features section, user admin tasks 80
file
  attaching, to blog entry 157, 158
FogBugz
  URL 170
footer message field, site information 243

G

group dashboard, Open Atrium 14, 88-90
groups
  about 11, 103
  accounting department, organizational
    chart 104
  archive option 117
  archiving 117
  background colors, modifying 114, 115
  blocked users, viewing 120
  Customize features section 112, 113

O

Open Atrium
about 10
blog 149
browser installation 51-56
browsers 22
calendar 193
features 12
files, downloading 48, 49
group 11
installing 46
intranet 11
Mac (MAMP) 47-49
page, URL 10
need for 18
site, setting up 47
subtheme, creating 278
system requirements 21
team spaces 11
URL 272
web server 21, 22
Windows (WAMP) 47-50

Open Atrium, features
blog 12
calendar 13
case tracker 17
document library 15
group dashboard 14
shoutbox 16

OpenID tab, user admin tasks 79
Organic groups (OG)
about 105
Accounting group 105
Accounts payable group 105
Accounts receivable group 105
Benefits group 105
Human Resources group 105
Payroll group 105
URL 105

P

performance page, routine maintenance
about 256
bandwidth optimizations 258
block cache 257

caching mode 256
cleared cache data 259
picture tab, user admin tasks 78, 79
private group 109
profile tab, user admin tasks 75-77
profile, user admin tasks 74, 75
projects tab, case tracker feature
about 184, 185
case, moving between projects 185
project, archiving 186-188
project, identifying 186
project, reactivating 188
public group
about 110
example 110
joining 122, 123
settings menu 111

R

**rebuild permissions, routine
maintenance 254, 255**
Reference this option 146
reorder menu
about 115, 116
icons, reordering 116
options 116
reporting
about 261
available updates page 261, 262
database logs 263
site status report 266, 267
resources
Drupal resources 269
revisions
about 134
highlight changes 136, 137
revisions tab 138, 139
subpages 139, 140
routine maintenance
about 248
cron 248
performance-caching 256
rebuilding permissions 254, 255
search indexing 250-254
site updates, applying 260

Thank you for buying
Drupal Intranets with Open Atrium

About Packt Publishing

Packt, pronounced 'packed', published its first book "*Mastering phpMyAdmin for Effective MySQL Management*" in April 2004 and subsequently continued to specialize in publishing highly focused books on specific technologies and solutions.

Our books and publications share the experiences of your fellow IT professionals in adapting and customizing today's systems, applications, and frameworks. Our solution based books give you the knowledge and power to customize the software and technologies you're using to get the job done. Packt books are more specific and less general than the IT books you have seen in the past. Our unique business model allows us to bring you more focused information, giving you more of what you need to know, and less of what you don't.

Packt is a modern, yet unique publishing company, which focuses on producing quality, cutting-edge books for communities of developers, administrators, and newbies alike. For more information, please visit our website: www.packtpub.com.

About Packt Open Source

In 2010, Packt launched two new brands, Packt Open Source and Packt Enterprise, in order to continue its focus on specialization. This book is part of the Packt Open Source brand, home to books published on software built around Open Source licences, and offering information to anybody from advanced developers to budding web designers. The Open Source brand also runs Packt's Open Source Royalty Scheme, by which Packt gives a royalty to each Open Source project about whose software a book is sold.

Writing for Packt

We welcome all inquiries from people who are interested in authoring. Book proposals should be sent to author@packtpub.com. If your book idea is still at an early stage and you would like to discuss it first before writing a formal book proposal, contact us; one of our commissioning editors will get in touch with you.

We're not just looking for published authors; if you have strong technical skills but no writing experience, our experienced editors can help you develop a writing career, or simply get some additional reward for your expertise.

Plone 3 Intranets

ISBN: 978-1-847199-08-9   Paperback: 312 pages

Design, build, and deploy a reliable, full-featured, and secure Plone-based enterprise intranet easily from scratch

1. Install, set up, and use a corporate Plone intranet with ease

2. Secure your intranet using Plone's out-of-the-box features

3. Explore the most useful add-ons for your intranet and learn how to use them

Liferay Portal 6 Enterprise Intranets

ISBN: 978-1-849510-38-7   Paperback: 692 pages

Build and maintain impressive corporate intranets with Liferay

1. Develop a professional Intranet using Liferay's practical functionality, usability, and technical innovation

2. Enhance your Intranet using your innovation and Liferay Portal's out-of-the-box portlets

3. Maximize your existing and future IT investments by optimizing your usage of Liferay Portal

Please check **www.PacktPub.com** for information on our titles

Drupal Web Services

ISBN: 978-1-849510-98-1   Paperback: 320 pages

Integrate social and multimedia Web services and applications with your Drupal Web site.

1. Explore different Web services and how they integrate with the Drupal CMS.

2. Reuse the applications without coding them again using the Web services protocols on your Drupal site.

3. Configure your Drupal site to consume various web services by using contributed Drupal modules for each specific task or application.

Drupal 7 Module Development

ISBN: 978-1-849511-16-2   Paperback: 420 pages

Create your own Drupal 7 modules from scratch

1. Specifically written for Drupal 7 development

2. Write your own Drupal modules, themes, and libraries

3. Discover the powerful new tools introduced in Drupal 7

Please check **www.PacktPub.com** for information on our titles

Drupal E-commerce with Ubercart 2.x

ISBN: 978-1-847199-20-1   Paperback: 364 pages

Build, administer, and customize an online store using Drupal with Ubercart

1. Create a powerful e-shop using the award-winning CMS Drupal and the robust e-commerce module Ubercart

2. Create and manage the product catalog and insert products in manual or batch mode

3. Apply SEO (search engine optimization) to your e-shop and adopt turn-key internet marketing techniques

Practical Plone 3: A Beginner's Guide to Building Powerful Websites

ISBN: 978-1-847191-78-6   Paperback: 592 pages

A beginner's practical guide to building Plone websites through graphical interface

1. Get a Plone-based website up and running quickly without dealing with code

2. Beginner's guide with easy-to-follow instructions and screenshots

3. Learn how to make the best use of Plone's out-of-the-box features

Please check **www.PacktPub.com** for information on our titles

CPSIA information can be obtained at www.ICGtesting.com
Printed in the USA
LVOW03s0110140614

389994LV00008B/63/P